The world expects parents to do a good job of raising the next generation to be healthy, happy and fulfilled members of society, and yet that same society offers no training for this essential and complex task. When things go wrong parents often feel guilty and helpless and do not know where to turn.

By telling the true stories of some of the families she has worked with in a Child and Family Clinic, Penny Jaques vividly and movingly describes a wide range of emotional problems and illustrates ways of thinking about family relationships which will help parents to understand and resolve some of the difficulties they may encounter in their own families.

This book sets out to help parents to find some new ways of understanding and tackling their children's emotional problems and the difficulties which often arise in family relationships.

To
David, Damian, Sophie and Daniel,
my family.

Understanding Children's Problems

Helping families to help themselves

PENNY JAQUES

UNWIN PAPERBACKS

London   Sydney

First published in Great Britain by Unwin® Paperbacks, an imprint
of Unwin Hyman Limited, in 1987

UNWIN HYMAN LIMITED
Denmark House, 37–39 Queen Elizabeth Street,
London SE1 2QB
and
40 Museum Street, London WC1A 1LU

Allen & Unwin Australia Pty Ltd
8 Napier Street, North Sydney, NSW 2060, Australia

Allen & Unwin New Zealand Ltd with the Port Nicholson Press,
60 Cambridge Terrace, Wellington, New Zealand

British Library Cataloguing in Publication Data

Jaques, Penny
    Understanding children's problems : helping
    families to help themselves.
    1. Child rearing   2. Parent and child
    I. Title
    306.8'74   QH769
    ISBN 0-04-649057-4

Set in 11 on 13 point Sabon by
V & M Graphics Ltd, Aylesbury, Bucks
and printed in Great Britain by
The Guernsey Press Co. Ltd, Guernsey, Channel Islands

Contents

Acknowledgements

Affectionate and warm thanks to the following: Anne Trudgill for the idea; Harriet Griffey for patient encouragement; Evelyn Tovey of 'Urchin' for efficient word processing and helpful suggestions; past and present members of my professional family in the St Albans Child and Family Clinic; and all the families who have so generously allowed me to tell their stories.

The quotation on page 15 from A. A. Milne is reproduced by permission of Methuen Children's Books.

Introduction

This is a book to help parents to find some new ways of thinking about family problems. We all have dreams of how family life could be but the reality often fails to live up to these hopes and longings. Bringing up children can be enriching, rewarding and great fun, but it can also be exhausting, baffling and very anxiety-provoking.

At one time or another most parents will be worried about some aspect of family life. Those who sail through the early years, coping with the exhausting demands of babies and small children, may find their teenagers bring them down with a crash. Others may find the early months and years a nightmare of doubt and worry and then thoroughly enjoy their children when they become more independent. There is little help available to prepare for the life-long job of being a parent. The one thing that we all will have had is the experience of having been a child and this will have a profound effect on our own attitudes to becoming parents. If parents had a happy childhood they may wish to recreate this for their children. If, for whatever reason, parents were unhappy in their original families they may have strong views about how they do not want it to be in their family. This can lead to difficulties, for as one parent said, 'It is all very well saying I don't want to be like my own mother, but then how shall I be?' She felt she was floundering.

When parents hit a bad patch with their children they may be touching on aspects of themselves which belong to their own early lives, for while the memories may have gone, or have become distorted with time, the feelings can linger on and be woken up by what is happening with the children. No one leaves their childhood self behind – it is incorporated into all later life experience and becoming a parent can rekindle aspects of the personality and emotions long forgotten or ignored. Many parents are surprised and alarmed when they get in touch with the emotions from childhood. 'I never had a bad temper until I had children' is a common protest. But as toddlers we have all experienced the passionate feelings which belong to that stage of development. How much we were allowed to give expression to such intense emotions will affect our ability as parents to deal with our small children in the turbulent 2-year-old phase.

When things go wrong in a family and a child is emotionally or behaviourally disturbed, the parents' confidence in their ability to help that child can dwindle away. They may need to get support and help. At such times parents often feel guilty as well as worried. It can be difficult to admit these feelings to close family and friends, however kind and supportive they may be. Teachers, family doctors, health visitors and many others in the caring professions may be able to counsel and advise and help to give parents back their confidence in their own ability to help their child. Sometimes reading books and magazines can be a source of help and understanding, particularly in explaining and defining what constitutes the 'normal' problems in children's emotional and social development.

Many emotional problems are resolved in the course of time and no one quite knows why, but sometimes the difficulties persist and then the advice to parents may well be 'to seek expert help'. At this point a lot of parents feel alarmed and bewildered. What sort of experts and what sort of help? Is their problem worth worrying about? Will they be criticised? What will happen? Does it help?

This book attempts to answer some of these questions by telling the true stories of some of the families that I have met in many years of working in a Child and Family Clinic. It highlights certain problems which can arise with children and their parents at various ages and stages, and illustrates how these problems can be understood and tackled in ways that can be used for many other sticking points in family relationships. I have not set out to make this an encyclopaedia of children's emotional difficulties, but my hope is that it provides sufficient variety for most parents to find something with which they can identify in their own experience of family life.

There are no magic cures which we who work in such clinics give to families, for the families have the solutions to their own problems. They are the real experts on themselves and all we can do is help them to find their way towards their own solutions. Somebody who is not emotionally involved can help the family to stand back and take a fresh look, so that things can be seen and understood which were previously confused and indistinct.

The families whose stories I am telling have been more than happy to give permission for me to include them in this book. They have all experienced various degrees of worry with their children and have expressed the hope that by sharing in this way other families may be helped. To those families who think they see part of their story here, but who I could not contact, be reassured that only you and I know that it is you. Names have been changed to preserve anonymity.

It is through sharing our hopes, fears and worries that we gain strength and the understanding which can lead to real happiness and joy. My thanks to all of you who have had the courage to acknowledge and face your problems. We have talked, played, cried and laughed together, and I have been greatly enriched and made much wiser by knowing everyone of you.

CHAPTER 1

What is a family?

Families come in a multitude of shapes and sizes, some seem to have walked out of a television advertisement: father, mother, son, daughter. Others are infinitely chaotic, having changed in structure many times in that family's life.

Some families live in groups of three or four generations, others have one grouping for part of the time and then change at weekends or holidays, when parents or some children from a previous relationship come and join in or go away. Some families are intricately bound together in a network of relatives, while others are isolated with no relatives and have to rely upon the resources within the family in order to meet all their emotional needs.

Asking some children the question 'Who is in your family?' will produce a list which takes in grandparents, aunts, uncles, cousins etc., all felt to be part of the family clan. Other children will find it hard to recall if they have any relatives outside their immediate family. This may be because they do not exist, but more often it is the result of unresolved splits and schisms which have occurred in previous generations.

There are many groups of adults and children who function as family units but in which the natural or legal bonds are vague or non-existent. Whatever the family set-up the children's most crucial need is to know who are their parents, natural or substitute, who make the decisions that affect their family's life and, last but far from least, to whom they can turn for their physical and emotional needs to be met.

Many children are confused and unhappy because the structure of their family group is muddled. Boundaries between generations can become blurred leaving children insecure and unsure about who is really in charge of them.

Family life-cycles

A family is a constantly changing social group with fluctuations of pressure from without and within. It changes shape and structure and makes subtle, or not so subtle, adaptations as it develops. This book is an exploration of the problems that can arise as families negotiate some of the more stressful periods of change.

Birth and death probably have the greatest impact on family life, but between these beginnings and endings there are other, perhaps less dramatic, events which can have a profound effect on the family. If we take a family as beginning with a couple who have chosen to live together in a one-to-one relationship then the arrival of the first baby can have a major impact on this unit, bringing as it does a sudden change from a two-person to a three-person structure. Triangles are not as comfortable or easy as twosomes and can often lead to upsets in which somebody feels left out. With the arrival of a second baby the family may achieve more of a balance between 'the parents' and 'the children'.

Parents usually feel more relaxed and confident coping with their second baby. But for the firstborn the arrival of this unknown and demanding intruder can lead to intense emotional distress. To have been the centre of the universe, the apple of the parents' eyes, and then suddenly to have to share that position must qualify as one of life's most demanding challenges.

Many of the stories which follow illustrate some of the difficulties that can arise later on in families if this early jealous rage has not found expression but become buried and distorted.

The second baby's arrival is not all bad news! Most children develop a deep love for the new baby and through the hurly-burly of family life learn to share and show concern for others, as well as how to cope with rivalry and the demands of living in a group – all good practice for becoming emotionally mature adults.

When a child starts school, the parents have to acknowledge the impingement of the outside world on family life and face the fact that the children are not totally dependent on them as parents. When the youngest child in a family starts school, the parent most involved in child care will probably have to make adjustments to fill a gap which will be created in his or her life. With adolescence comes the challenge to the parents' authority and the struggle for increasing independence.

Then the children leave home and the parents in middle age are back in a one-to-one relationship which may have changed over the years. It is a time to take stock of their lives. It is also at about this time that grandparents may become more dependent. When the grandparents die, parents may themselves become grandparents, involving as it does a change in attitude to children who are now parents themselves. The cycle has come right round.

Within the family each individual is making a personal journey towards maturity. Stress and strain on the family, whenever and wherever it comes, will have a different impact on each member, depending on which stage of development each has reached. When thinking about an individual child's emotional problem it is important to look at where the whole family is in its life-cycle, to put that child's problem into context and understand what the symptom means both in terms of the whole family's current and past experience and the individual child's personal history and stage of emotional development.

What is a problem?

Deciding whether a problem is worth worrying about can be part of the problem. Some parents tolerate behaviour in their children which would send other parents straight up the wall! The concepts of 'normal' and 'abnormal' are impossible to apply to the ups and downs of children's emotional development and to family life in general. We can make general statements such as that it is normal for infants to cry, for toddlers to have temper tantrums, for exam candidates to worry, for teenagers to be rebellious, but deciding whether the infant is crying too much or the toddler having too many tantrums, and so on, seems to require a yardstick that does not exist. Parents are usually the best judge of whether there is a problem. They know, and care, about their children more than anyone else and a worried parent should be listened to and have access to help.

Children's emotional development is never smooth – there are so many influences on a child from within and without, and all need to be taken account of in understanding why problems emerge along the way. One stage in development follows another, but the progress may not be smooth and often a child will go back a step when under stress for whatever reason. Slipping back into an earlier and safer way of behaving is not just a phenomenon of childhood, we all do it from time to time when under particular stress. It is when a child cannot recover from the temporary setback but seems to get stuck in an earlier stage of development that parents are right to be concerned.

This book is not about the problems as such, but rather about ways of thinking creatively around them, so leading to growth and change. Nevertheless, it may be helpful to list some of the sorts of symptoms of upset that bring families for help. It cannot be a complete list, because there are as many worries as there are children, but here are just some of the signs of emotional distress.

Sleep disturbance	Soiling
Excessive crying	Depression
Eating problems	Suicidal thoughts
Shyness	Stealing
Aggressive behaviour	School refusal
Temper tantrums	Anxiety

Separation anxiety   Delinquency
Fears   Psychosomatic illness
Bullying, or being bullied   Hyperactivity
Wetting   Inability to concentrate

It is important to stress that any of these behaviours can occur at particularly difficult or upsetting times in the life of a child or its family – changes in routine, separations, illness, changes in the environment, such as going to a new school, moving house, the arrival of a new baby, or the creation of a new family – all these and many others are reasons why children revert to behaviour which they may have left behind. It is when the problem persists and is making the child and family worried and upset that parents may need help to see the problem in a new way which can lead to change and recovery. I hope that the true stories which make up this book will help parents towards some new understandings of family problems.

Why take a family approach?

In recent years, there has been a revolution in the approach to helping children who have emotional problems. More and more agencies are taking a family-based approach for it is widely accepted that it is within the context of the family group that each of us develops our sense of who we are, how we feel about ourselves and others, and our ability to fit into the world. What happens to each of us as we grow through infancy and childhood to adolescence and adulthood will, for better or worse, profoundly influence our emotional and social development.

When one child in a family becomes emotionally upset that upset is a communication which needs to be understood, a signpost or symptom drawing attention to underlying distress which can find no other means of expression. In a family group the individual members, from the oldest to the youngest, are like cogs which are synchronised in such a way that the family wheel can keep turning and move along in its own unique way. Change in one cog will affect the others whether they like it or not and because change is often painful and upsets the rhythm of family life, the family will exert all sorts of pressures on the individual cog to fit back into place. In order for that cog or family member to grow and develop all the other cogs will need to change too.

This is why people who treat troubled children usually prefer to work with the whole family rather than seeing the child alone.

It is often the case that the child who is presented as the one who has or is 'the problem' may be drawing attention to more serious, although hidden, difficulties between other members of the family, often the parents. Once these are acknowledged and the parents begin to work together to improve their relationship, the child is released from his job as standard bearer for the family's distress and no longer has to have or be the problem.

Sometimes the worry or difficult behaviour simply disappears after one family meeting. It seems as if the experience of all sitting down together to listen to everyone's point of view and taking the problem seriously is in itself a healing process. How often in normal family life do parents and children of varying ages get together to share a worry without being interrupted by telephone, front-door bell, TV and all the other distractions of modern life?

One of the main themes running through the stories that follow is that families can heal themselves of a great deal of emotional pain that is often self-inflicted. Things go wrong in families when there is poor communication and individual members become confused about their own and others longings and expectations. Time spent confronting what are sometimes difficult and painful feelings can lead to creative change and the growth of love which is not conditional upon a strict adherence to family rules and expectations but acknowledges and celebrates each family member as valuable and unique.

CHAPTER 2

Setting the scene

All the families whose stories I tell in this book came to a clinic called the Child and Family Clinic. Up and down the country there are similar clinics which may vary in name and structure. The title, 'Child Guidance Clinic' is probably the most widely known, but some clinics are called 'Child and Family Psychiatric Clinics' and in hospitals they may be called 'Departments of Child Psychiatry'. Some come under the education authority, others under health, and there are voluntary agencies who also offer a similar service (see Chapter 19).

Procedures for referral may vary too. Where I work we have an open referral system so that parents can get in touch direct without having to get a letter from another professional. This encourages parents to seek help for themselves and their families before a problem becomes too entrenched. The earlier a worry is dealt with the better for the child, the family and the whole community. Many adults who seek help from doctors, psychiatrists, marriage guidance counsellors, or other professional helpers in the community, are still suffering from the unresolved problems of childhood. If they had only had access to help when they were young a great deal of emotional pain and psychiatric illness could have been avoided. Child Guidance Clinics are there to be used by ordinary families with ordinary worries as well as for the more seriously disturbed children and their families.

Clinics are staffed by multidisciplinary teams of workers, drawn from different professional groups. These teams vary both in size and structure from one area to another, but will probably include the following categories of workers.

A *Child Psychiatrist* is a medically qualified doctor who has a post-graduate qualification in adult psychiatry and has then specialised in child and adolescent psychiatry.

A *Clinic Social Worker* is a qualified and experienced social worker with a special interest in therapeutic work with parents and children. Many have undertaken further training in this area.

A *Child Psychotherapist* has completed a post-graduate training in understanding and treating emotionally disturbed children and adolescents. An essential part of training for this one-to-one work with children is to have had a personal psychoanalysis.

An Educational Psychologist has a psychology degree and is a qualified and experienced teacher who has undertaken post-graduate training in educational psychology. The educational psychologist can advise school staff and parents on a child's learning, emotional or behavioural problems manifest in school.

Among the other professionals who work in clinic teams are Play Therapists, Art Therapists, Clinical Psychologists, Remedial Teachers and Educational Therapists. Hospital departments of Child Psychiatry and Adolescent Units will have in-patient beds and the full range of medical, paramedical and teaching staff.

Although clinic staff have arrived from these varied professional roots, they come together with a shared interest in, and commitment to, understanding troubled children and families. Many of us are drawn to this field of work because we have personal experience of family disruption or problems when we were young. It is therefore very important that both during and after training we have opportunities to look closely at the feelings within us about what has happened, so that we do not confuse our own emotions and attitudes with those of the families who come to us for help.

When a family first comes to the clinic our hope is that by taking a family-based approach we shall be able to help the family resolve the problem quite quickly, particularly if the difficulty is of short duration. But there are times when parents welcome a chance to talk about their worries without the children being present. It is important and helpful for children to know that there are boundaries within the family and moments when their parents actually or metaphorically 'close the bedroom door'.

Some children have emotional problems which cannot be understood and resolved through an approach which focuses solely on family interaction and relationships. They will need the special skills and training of the child psychiatrist and child psychotherapist who can treat individual children on a one-to-one basis, to explore the meaning and origin of the child's problems through regular sessions over a period of time. The parents of a child in individual therapy will also need regular support and help to understand the difficulties and adjust to the changes in their child which may result from psychotherapy. So although individual psychotherapy is not the subject or focus of this book, it is important to stress that it is a valuable part of the service offered by Child Guidance Clinics.

Play as communication

Lots of things go on in a family session apart from talking. Children often communicate through their play and for this reason there are always certain toys available in the clinic, the most important and useful of these are paper, coloured pencils and paint, a dolls' house complete with family members and furniture, and sets of domestic and wild animals. Plasticine is a wonderful material for expressing feelings – it can be modelled, cut, bashed and squashed, and objects can be endlessly remade. The other day I was with a family whose 6-year-old boy was anxious and clinging and hated to leave his mother's side to go to school. While his parents talked he made a series of plasticine babies, and then took great delight in cutting off their heads, a clear communication about his envy for the one year old who could stay with mum all day, and quite a revelation in a boy who had shown no overt signs of jealousy and was described as 'devoted to the baby'. Through his play he was showing his hidden feelings. How children play in the dolls' house will reveal a lot about what goes on both at home, and in the inner world of the child. One little girl, who was prone to sudden very violent outbursts of rage, insisted on tidying the dolls' house. She put each piece of furniture against the wall and separated the dolls so there was only one family member in each room. It looked lifeless and overcontrolled and seemed to be communicating this child's view of the problem her family had in getting on well when they were all together and her own anxiety about trying to control events.

Children of all ages love playing with toy animals, domestic and wild ones, and their play can give clues about how they are feeling. A 5-year-old boy arranged the domestic animals inside a fence and put the wild creatures outside. He seemed to be indicating that there was a threat to his security, which I subsequently learned was actually the case. The wild animals can be used by children to give expression to their own wild and passionate feelings. Another 5 year old took six crocodiles and hippopotami and put them in the dolls' house where the daddy doll was positioned watching the television. He put the wild animals in a circle surrounding the daddy doll and then stood back gleefully. The message was about how much this little boy wanted to keep his father from going to work and he was not the only one who was angry about his father's unavailability. When his mother saw the set-up in the dolls' house, she commented ruefully that six crocs and three hippos wouldn't stop her husband working too hard. The little boy was expressing something for himself, his mother, and the rest of the family. It was a crucial communication, for it led to a shift in focus from the child as the problem to the father's unavailability.

The first time Sharon came to the clinic with her family she went straight over to the dolls' house and found a baby doll which she then 'injected' with a sharp pencil. Sharon, then 7, had spent several months in hospital when she was only one. She had suffered great pain and acute distress. Her parents had stayed with her as much as possible but could not hold or cuddle her. Through her play Sharon gave direct expression to the feelings about all that had happened to her. She dealt with the overwhelming helplessness and fear by becoming the one who inflicted 'the treatment' on the dolls. She could not talk directly about what had happened – she probably had few real memories, but she put a lot of words into the dolls' mouths and through her play she was able to face the buried fears and begin to recover.

The significance of painting and drawing

For most children the sight of a large piece of clean paper and a box of crayons, felt-tip pens or paints is irresistible. In the clinic we always have these items ready for a family session, not as a means of 'keeping the children occupied' but to provide another sort of communication which can sometimes direct and always enrich and give more meaning to the discussion.

I recently saw a family where the father had died only a few months earlier, leaving three young children. The eldest, a girl of 9, was being aggressive and demanding with her mother who was unable to tolerate the behaviour while she was herself feeling so grief-stricken. As we all talked the little girl drew a colourful and lively drawing of a girl (herself) skipping in a field full of flowers. The sun was shining and the drawing was full of joy. Then gradually she added a cloud and blacked out the sun, and with a grey wax crayon covered the whole picture with large drops of rain, the tears which up to then she had not been able to shed.

It may not be what the child paints but how he paints and what he thinks about his painting which is important. In the stories which make up this book I give a number of examples which illustrate the significance of children's artistic creations.

There are children who cannot allow themselves the freedom of self-expression and will not dare to pick up a brush or put a mark onto paper. Perhaps the child is responding to strict rules from parents about being clean and tidy, or maybe he is inhibited and anxious about the self-exposure involved. He may already have a sense that nothing he produces is any good, so he no longer tries. Some children will take a large sheet of paper and draw a tiny figure in one corner. This may be a way of saying how small and insignificant the child feels. At the other extreme is the child who paints without enough control, so that easel, floor, walls and himself get covered. In a 2 year old that would be normal, but in a much older child it might indicate that he had not yet developed enough self-control and this could be causing problems in other aspects of his life.

The content of a drawing or painting can be very helpful in understanding the inner world of a child and his views of important people and events in his life. In Chapter 7, Sarah's zoo picture was a way of introducing her father into the family session although she had not seen him for two years.

A 14 year old who could not speak about his anxieties drew an ugly self-portrait, a punk-like face quite unlike his own gentle, sensitive features. He covered it with exploding spots, and wrote on the head 'crazy', 'mad', 'bad' and inside the chest he drew a bottle of fizzy pop exploding. He spoke not one word but his drawing conveyed quite clearly his fear of going mad and his sense of being full of emotions and impulses which were bottled up and he feared were going to explode.

A 4 year old who was unable to leave her mother's side came with her family for a first meeting and immediately drew a large house, complete with front door and windows. It was only on closer inspection that I noticed four tiny wheels supporting the house. I asked her about the wheels. She grinned and looked straight at her mother, who laughed and said, 'That's me, I am always saying I wish our house had wheels, then I could go out and stay in at the same time.' The whole family laughed. The 4 year old had drawn a picture of the family's real problem which was the mother's agoraphobia. The little girl's separation anxiety could now clearly be understood as an extension of her mother's difficulty.

Jason would draw by the hour at home and when his parents showed their genuine interest in what he had created he would tear up his drawings saying they were no good. His parents had tried reasoning with him to try convincing him that they thought his drawings were good, which in fact they were, but they could get nowhere and his self-esteem was at rock bottom. It was important for his parents to hear Jason's real communication which was, '*I* am feeling no good, so nothing I do can feel any good.' To have told him not to be so silly would have confirmed Jason even further in his view that he was silly and stupid. They needed to reassure Jason of his worth to them and to question themselves about whether he was under too much pressure to be 'good' in various areas of his life.

Seven-year-old Sam sat in the classroom and at home sucking his thumb and gazing into space. He came to the clinic with his mother, stepfather and lively 2-year-old sister. He refused to play or draw, preferring to sit curled up on a chair with his thumb in his mouth. On the family's third visit he slid quietly out of his chair, went over to the table and with a red wax crayon drew an enormous shark. It was the most ferocious creature imaginable with massive pointed teeth protruding from its open jaws. It looked as though it could leap out of the page and attack us all. Sam had allowed us a glimpse of the powerful, dangerous feelings which he only managed to keep under control by staying silent and withdrawn. It was significant that Sam's father had been a violent man and when Sam's mother had remarried she chose a very quiet and gentle person. She made a vow that she would never again allow anyone in the family to become aggressive and told me with pride that in their family there was never a cross word. Sam was not free to express any angry feelings at all and the family had to do a lot of work before they all felt safe enough for Sam to be himself.

Ben's output of dinosaurs was prodigious, though he was only 5 years old he could draw them by the yard – the fire-breathing, gnashing-teeth variety. With his baby brother he was angelic, never lost his temper and showed a high degree of tenderness and care. Ben's parents understood that his drawings provided an essential outlet for his envious rage and they were glad he could give expression to them in such a creative way.

CHAPTER 3

Sleep deprivation

A well-known torture

Preparing for the arrival of a new baby takes a great deal of physical and emotional energy. It is vitally important that the experience of childbirth should, wherever possible, be one which allows both mother and infant to establish a mutually satisfying relationship. Some new mothers feel an intense attachment to their newborn infant while others take some days, weeks or even months to feel what they expected or hoped they would feel. The actual experience of childbirth may help or hinder this attachment, but what happens afterwards is crucial too.

It is very hard to prepare for the time after the arrival of the baby. Most new parents expect to feel tired for a few weeks while feeding and sleeping rhythms are established, but it comes as a dreadful shock when they find that their infant will not sleep.

Sleep deprivation is a well-known torture. A baby who will not sleep and cries endlessly can soon feel like a torturer. Parents get exhausted, patience wears thin, tempers flare up and parents feel inadequate and helpless. Before long everyone feels they are in the middle of an endless nightmare. The physical effects of being exhausted are bad enough, but for a lot of parents it is the emotional difficulties that are the worst of all.

Some babies settle into a regular sleeping/waking pattern effortlessly, others may take a few weeks, but many continue to have sleeping difficulties for months or years. Most mothers coping with a sleepless infant feel dreadful, marriages can reach breaking point and self-esteem may hit rock bottom. For many women it may be the first time in their lives they have felt so inadequate, upset and angry. Then there is the guilt. Guilt about feeling such a failure. Guilt at seeing a partner leaving for work with grey bags under his eyes, but worst of all the guilt at feeling so angry towards the baby who seems to be the cause of so much upset.

It always seems that everyone else's baby sleeps contentedly! All babies out in their prams seem to be asleep. Babies in magazines and on advertisements are asleep or if they are awake they look relaxed and contented. There is an awful sense of isolation for parents awake all night. When a colleague and I organised an open meeting to discuss sleep problems we were amazed to see the room packed with mothers and babies. Out of this meeting we ran a series of small groups to share the problem and the first thing the members of these groups commented on was the relief at not being the only one. They pooled their experiences of being up and down all night feeding, rocking, leaving the baby to cry, picking him up, playing with him, shouting at him and giving him medicine (which hardly ever works), putting toys in his cot, taking them away again, bringing him into the parents' bed, patting his back, sometimes even putting him in the car and going for a drive until he drops off, only to wake up and scream when the engine is turned off. All the parents in our sleep groups felt they understood why some people hit their babies. They could feel their own self-control running very thin and acknowledged that arguments with partners were often the only way to get their feelings out with some degree of safety.

Family life in such circumstances may get off to a bad start but there are ways of tackling the problem. Here are two true stories of how two very different families solved their babies' sleeping problems.

Jenny was a single mother of 20 whose Health Visitor suggested she came for help with Paul who was 13 months. Paul had never slept well and for several weeks Jenny was getting less than four hours sleep a night and that was always broken by Paul's crying. We met once and I was struck by how totally worn out they both appeared to be. Jenny said she was afraid she was going to have a breakdown and could not cope any longer.

Jenny lived with her mother and grandmother. Grandmother was very old and had come to live with them shortly before Paul was born. She criticised Jenny constantly, accusing her of cruelty if she ever let Paul cry. Jenny's mother had been a great support and ever since Paul was a tiny baby had helped in all sorts of ways, particularly in the evenings when Jenny wanted to go out. Sadly, Jenny's mother had become ill and needed a major operation which left her unable to lift Paul. She was so tired by the evenings that Jenny feared burdening her and making her ill again. Paul was obviously upset and puzzled by his Nan no longer spending time with him. Jenny felt guilty that she and Paul were a burden, while in the background grandmother was waiting to complain. So Jenny and I worked out a plan. We agreed that she would not try to put it into action until she felt ready, and that she would need her mother's full co-operation. I thought it might take about a week to get Paul to sleep and I warned that it would be a strain on them all in the short term.

The overall plan was designed to help Paul to learn the difference between day and night. To know for certain that whatever happened he would not be taken downstairs after bedtime. Jenny used to bath Paul in the morning but we planned to move this to the evening. Jenny had been keeping him downstairs to play with him to try and make him tired, but it seemed to have had the opposite effect. When she had put him in his cot he had refused to lie down and before long she had brought him down for more play. In the night she had often taken him into her bed but he never settled and again she would be up and down all night. She could barely control her anger and with no partner to share the burden, as well as the worries over her mother, this situation felt desperate.

The plan included Jenny's mother. They were to agree not to let grandmother's comments upset them. The plan also included a short playtime for Paul and Jenny's mother, with Jenny around to lift and help when necessary. Jenny was to ask her mother to be quite honest about how much she could manage. Paul would then have a bath followed by a bedtime drink which Jenny would give him in his room. Jenny was going to find a small electric fire and a comfortable chair for herself to put in his room. She was to help Paul wind down from the day, keeping her voice quiet and the light low, and refuse his invitations to play. Then she would lay him down in his cot, making sure he was warmly dressed so that if he climbed out of his covers he would not be cold. She would have already moved the pile of toys out of his cot, leaving only his favourite cuddly toy. She was to kiss him 'goodnight' calmly and walk, not tiptoe, out of the room and go downstairs. We both knew that the first night would be the worst so we planned for every eventuality and wrote the plan down for Jenny to pin on the wall. When Paul cried Jenny would leave him for ten minutes and then she would go calmly into his room and keeping her voice low would gently lay him down, stroke his back for a minute or two and then go downstairs. If he cried again she would repeat the pattern, so even on this first night he would be learning that although his mother was there she would not be taking him downstairs or playing with him.

On the second night the routine was exactly the same except that Jenny would wait twenty minutes before going up to Paul when he cried. The next night it would be thirty minutes and the next an hour. Of course, Jenny could decide at any time that Paul's crying was becoming so frantic that she would go to him earlier. In which case, she would pick him up for a reassuring cuddle but not play or stay in the room for more than a couple of minutes.

To reinforce the difference between day and night we planned that when Jenny put him up for his daytime rests he would have his toys in the cot, and when Jenny decided he could get up she would go in to him talking in a normal daytime voice and take him downstairs to get on with the day.

Of course, it is easy to make a plan like this in the cold light of day. We both knew it would feel very different in the small hours when Jenny longed to sleep and would be feeling impatient and angry. I reassured her that if the plan collapsed she could always start again. I stressed that *she* was going to be in charge of what happened in the night and that would help Paul to become less anxious.

The final part of the plan was that Jenny would telephone me each morning to tell me in detail what had happened the previous night. To my surprise she telephoned the very next morning. She had managed the plan down to the smallest detail and Paul had woken frequently, but she had resisted the temptation to take him down to the warm living-room where Jenny and her mother were enjoying a play on television. Having the plan pinned on the door of Paul's room had helped Jenny to stick at it. The next night he woke only four hourly and the third night he slept for ten hours without waking. Jenny laughingly admitted she had lain awake wondering if she should go in to check he was all right! She had felt quite triumphant and confident that she would be able to cope if the problem recurred. Jenny now felt she was in charge of Paul and not the other way round. She had broken the vicious circle of anxious waking and crying and Paul and she could begin to enjoy life together.

In contrast to Jenny, Rhoda and Charles lived in a luxuriously converted cottage full of expensive antiques and every kind of labour-saving device. Rhoda had been a successful civil servant and Charles was a solicitor with an expanding and busy practice. They had decided to wait to have children until they had had several years to concentrate on their careers, get their home as they wanted it and enjoy the freedom of foreign travel and trips to concerts and theatres. To their surprise and disappointment Rhoda did not conceive a baby at the time they planned. Rhoda gave up work hoping her more relaxed life would help her become pregnant. As time passed the tension increased and Rhoda became more and more depressed. Their previously enjoyable sex life lost its spontaneity as they tried to find the best time to conceive. At the fertility clinic nothing abnormal could be discovered and then, just after Rhoda had asked for her job back, she became pregnant. She was now 39 and Charles

42 and they were over the moon with excitement. Rhoda attended ante-natal classes and read everything she could lay her hands on about baby and child care. She had a long exhausting labour but a normal delivery and Emily was a beautiful and healthy baby.

Rhoda had difficulties breast-feeding Emily but was determined to be successful and put up with a lot of pain for some days. Her persistence paid off and she established a mutually enjoyable feeding pattern and Emily flourished. Neither Rhoda nor Charles could bear to hear Emily cry. They picked her up immediately day or night and Rhoda would stop whatever she was doing to feed Emily. The months passed and Rhoda began to wonder if she and Charles would ever have any time to themselves. Emily was always there and she cried whenever she was put down, even for a minute. She was becoming a rather miserable baby but Rhoda hoped she might be happier when she could crawl around. This did not happen. Emily was unhappy day and night and Rhoda was becoming depressed. Like many parents of sleepless babies, Rhoda and Charles tried everything before they asked for help and I felt it was significant that when Rhoda telephoned me she asked to see me without Charles. She was worried that he was nearly at breaking point and she wanted to protect him from the problem. I told her that Emily's not sleeping was a problem for them both and I thought it was important to meet both parents when there were problems in the family. Rhoda discussed this with Charles and was surprised by his positive attitude about being included.

When I arrived at their beautiful home Rhoda looked worn out but had gone to a lot of trouble grinding fresh coffee beans and offering me home-made biscuits. Charles was a warm and friendly person who did not look as though he was missing any sleep. Emily was a crotchety one year old who rejected whatever her parents offered and looked pale and tired. As Charles and Rhoda talked I could begin to understand why they were finding it so hard to cope.

Rhoda's father had been a famous musician, her mother a published author. From an early age Rhoda's role in the family had been to look after her sister Alison who was six years younger, while her parents pursued their careers. Rhoda had become quite possessive about Alison and recalled her feelings of annoyance and anger when, as she saw it, her mother interfered. She had very few memories of her father joining in family life. She could remember having to tiptoe past his door in order not to interfere with his practice.

Charles was an only child cared for by a trained nanny when he was small and he went to boarding school from the age of 7. When he was 12 his parents separated and he spent school holidays going from one to the other. His childhood daydream had been to have a 'real' family with brothers and sisters.

So here were two people deeply committed to each other and each with a dream about what family life could be like, but the dream was being spoiled.

I asked them how it made them feel when Emily began to cry. For Rhoda it was the proof that she was not the successful mother she thought she should be. For Charles it felt as if Emily must feel abandoned and lonely as he had felt when he was young. When Rhoda spoke of having to care for her sister, I wondered out loud what she had done with her resentful angry feelings about having to be a mother for Alison. It was difficult for Rhoda to acknowledge these buried feelings but she began to remember times when she had wanted to hurt Alison and had made her cry. She said there had been moments with Emily when she had been frightened that she might hurt her. At these moments she made extra efforts to be kind and loving. It seemed that Rhoda was afraid to let any angry feelings come out lest she be overwhelmed and do something awful.

As we talked Charles told Rhoda how helpless he felt in the face of Emily's demands. He longed to help but did not know what to do and Rhoda had always seemed to him to be so capable. She then realised she had been treating Charles just as if he were her father; someone who must be protected from the demands of family life. Charles was able to tell her of his willingness to share the parenting, not just the good bits but the sleepless nights too. When he said this Rhoda cried with relief and for the first time for weeks she let him comfort her.

Then we could make a plan, rather similar to the one Jenny and I had drawn up. I asked them to think of a realistic goal to aim for. They discussed this with obvious pleasure and agreed they would like to be able to have a whole evening together without Emily being with them. Rhoda would cook a special meal and Charles would open a bottle of expensive wine which had been languishing in the cellar waiting for a suitable celebration. There were several stages to be worked through to achieve this goal.

Rhoda had always believed that a 'good' mother would have her baby tucked up in bed before father came home. Charles had been unable to say that he would like to have time with Emily before she went to bed. He admitted that he had often been secretly pleased that Emily had refused to settle in the evening so that he could play with her. Not surprising that Emily had made sure she stayed awake! They now agreed that Charles would put Emily to bed having looked at picture books and played quietly in her room. He would call Rhoda when Emily was ready to be settled. They would then say goodnight and go downstairs. If she stayed awake but did not cry they would leave her. If she cried for more than ten minutes Charles would take responsibility for settling her but would not play with her or take her out of her cot. During the night if Emily woke Rhoda would go on the first occasion but Charles would take his turn if necessary later on. To Rhoda's surprise he was happy to do this. The plan involved extending the time they left her to cry each night. They decided not to start the routine until they had been back for a week after a weekend away which they knew would disrupt Emily.

They achieved their goal in five nights and in the process consolidated their relationship. Rhoda learned that it was good to share responsibility and Charles discovered he knew more about parenting than he thought he did. Rhoda gave herself permission to want to be without Emily sometimes. Emily, though most put out at first that she could not join in all the fun, became more relaxed and contented when she felt her parents anxiety had diminished and they were settling her in a way that made her feel safe.

Shortly after this Rhoda found an elderly woman in the village who was delighted to babysit, and to their surprise Rhoda and Charles found it was possible to go out and enjoy themselves without feeling guilty and worried.

As an afterthought, it is worth reminding anyone with a sleepless baby that in a few years that baby will have turned into an adolescent who never gets out of bed! But that is another story.

CHAPTER 4

'He's just trying to show me up'

Stephen: A rebellious 3 year old

Every parent knows that having a toddler around is a more than full-time job. The child, delighted with his newfound mobility and developing sense of independence, explores the world with never-ending energy and enthusiasm and conflict is bound to arise when parents have to set limits. When thwarted, a toddler is a force to be reckoned with and how a parent reacts to a child in a full-blown temper tantrum will depend partly on circumstances, but also on the feelings that are evoked in the parent by such an intense outburst of passion.

Learning self-discipline is a long, slow process and comes about gradually as the young child's wish to please his parents overrides his urge to do his own thing. But some parents cannot bear it when their child ignores their attempts to control him and fear that unless they immediately win this battle of wills, their tiny rebellious child will grow into a large rebellious teenager. In their anxiety to gain control of the situation, they may react in an angry and retaliatory way, which leaves them distressed and guilty.

There is plenty of sensible advice available these days which encourages parents to adopt a low-key approach in engaging children to co-operate over such things as toilet training, but many parents cannot follow this advice because they get into battle with their small children, which stir up feelings in them of which they are normally unaware. When these emotions surface they can get in the way of the parents more mature and coping side. A mother whose child is resisting her every attempt to get his co-operation over potty training may be dealing, among other things, with a fear of criticism. At a conscious level she may worry about the critical comments and attitudes of relatives and neighbours. At a deeper level she may fall victim to her own internal judge. Many people set themselves impossibly high standards, based on their own parents' expectations of them when they were small. When they feel they are falling short of these high standards they become very anxious and try to reduce the anxiety by getting everything and everyone under control. It is this fear of failure at the deepest level that can make matters worse and contribute to the parents increasing sense of not being able to cope with the everyday ups and downs of life with a small child.

Parents who were never allowed as children to give vent to their own angry feelings, and learnt at a very early age to be obedient and overcontrolled, find it intolerable when their own small children come out with the forbidden behaviours. They see their child trying to get away with something that they could never have achieved, and which must therefore be stopped. The scene is set for an ongoing battle in which everyone ends up frustrated and angry. The story which follows illustrates some of these issues, in particular the power of the past to be alive in the present, and to interfere in the parent's capacity to deal with the problems of young children.

Moira's health visitor telephoned me about Stephen, who would not eat, fought his mother over everything and was impossible to take out of the house because he refused to stay in his pushchair or hold his mother's hand. He seemed to her to take pleasure in doing the exact opposite from what she had asked him, and she was at the end of her tether and afraid that she would harm him. The health visitor had reassured Moira that Stephen was a normal healthy child and had given Moira good advice on how to de-escalate the battles with Stephen, none of which Moira had been able to put into practice. The health visitor had been to see Stephen in his playgroup, where he was absolutely no trouble. 'He's a smashing little chap,' was the leader's comment, and she found it hard to believe that he was being a problem. Stephen's father, Derek, was a senior fire officer and Moira, who had been a secretary, was not working at that time. There was a daughter, Sharon, who was 7 when I first met the family.

I went to see them at home and was immediately struck by a number of things. Derek seemed very laid back and said there really was no problem and he could not understand why Moira found Stephen so difficult, for he could manage him quite easily. Sharon was a shy, quiet 7 year old who sat on the settee throughout my visit. Her parents said this was quite usual and Moira said more than once to her, 'You are mummy's good girl, aren't you?'

Stephen, on the other hand, was full of beans. He would play on the floor, run out of the room to fetch things and come and show me objects, and even try to get into my handbag. Moira got more and more flustered and angry, while Derek sat back and watched. Moira would say, in a tense voice, '*Don't* touch the TV, Stephen', and of course Stephen went straight on pushing the knobs. The tension mounted and Moira and Stephen got further entrenched in their battle positions. Everything Moira said began with the word 'don't' and with a triumphant gleam in his eye, Stephen 'did'. Moira turned to me in desperation saying that she knew Stephen was just trying to show her up, to humiliate her, and that was why she could not take him out because she was unable to control him and people were always looking critically at her. At this point Stephen decided to play upstairs and then Moira poured out her feelings about Stephen not eating. The battles at mealtimes could go on for up to two hours. Sometimes Moira admitted she had tied Stephen's hands to the chair and forced the food into his mouth, but he only spat it out. When Derek was around Stephen ate quite happily and so this compounded Moira's sense of failure, frustration and anger. She spoke of her real terror that Stephen might die if he did not eat. It was quite obvious to me that Stephen was an active, healthy and sturdy little boy, so this worry of Moira's had to have other meanings. I also wanted to understand why Derek was so backward in coming forward to rescue his wife, when she was in such a desperate state. I arranged to see them again, this time without the children.

As a couple they seemed comfortable together and Moira was noticeably more relaxed. We talked about their early lives and I was deeply moved by what I heard. It felt as if a strong beam of light was falling on all the confusion and pain that I had witnessed on my first visit. What I heard confirmed for me the power of the past to be alive in the present. Of how the feelings that belonged to people and events in the past can spill over and confuse current relationships.

I had been wondering who Stephen represented for Moira. Most 2 to 3 year olds can be very exhausting and defiant, but it was Moira's sense that Stephen was constantly trying to humiliate her that seemed irrational, and it was this aspect of the whole situation that had brought Moira to breaking point. As she spoke about her own childhood, it was obvious that Derek had never heard the full story and he listened, amazed.

Moira was the second daughter of married parents. They lived in the country in Scotland and for as long as she could remember she had been the Cinderella of the family, made to work in the home, to shop, cook and mend, while her older sister was indulged and spoiled. Nothing Moira did was right. Her mother often hit her, on occasions very severely. Her father, though more gentle, never once intervened to rescue her. Once she ran into the village and told someone what was happening to her, but she was not really believed and told to 'be a good girl and go home'. She had no doubt that she was a victim of serious child abuse and thought it likely that had these events occurred today, she would have been offered help much sooner. All through this ghastly childhood she puzzled and wondered why she was so often punished. She tried to please her mother and failed. She developed a deep down sense that she must be no good and she felt trapped and helpless. As soon as she was 16 she left home and never returned. Through her own efforts and determination she coped with life, thankful to have put the nightmare in the past. She met Derek when they worked together and when they married she was happier than she could have hoped. She saw nothing of her mother, but when she was pregnant with Sharon she decided the time was right to make contact. She felt that perhaps there was a tiny chance that her memories were wrong, that her mother after all could love and value her, that there might have been hope of some forgiveness. Moira wrote to her mother telling her she was pregnant but heard nothing. Sharon's birth was difficult. After a long labour Moira had a caesarian delivery. A few hours after that her mother walked into the hospital. Almost her first comment when she heard what had happened was, 'Trust you, you couldn't even get *that* right, could you?' Moira felt like screaming at her mother to get out but she remained calm, the visit was brief and they never met again. Moira had never once in her life told her mother how she felt.

Having heard this awful story, I understood who Stephen was for Moira. He was the replacement for her mother, the taunting, humiliating persecutor. To an outsider he was, of course, just a normal, bright inquisitive and rather exhausting 3 year old. To Moira he was the reincarnation of her abusing mother. All through her childhood she had dealt with her anger towards her parents by convincing herself that it must all be *her* fault. She never retaliated or exploded, and so the feelings of injustice, pain and rage were pushed down like a fizzy drink in a bottle. Stephen's provocative behaviour released the cork, and out came Moira's murderous rage, bottled up for years with the pressure having increased all the time. No wonder she felt afraid that she might kill Stephen. There were still some missing bits of the puzzle. Why was Derek leaving Moira to get deeper and deeper into difficulties and why did Moira not welcome his help? And why was she so obsessed with the idea that Stephen would die if he did not eat every single thing that she gave him?

Derek's childhood could not have been more different. He was the fourth of sixteen children. He recalled a happy childhood with very clear, strict rules about right and wrong. Mother was in charge and kept a cane in every room, which Derek could not ever remember her using. Being one of the eldest he often helped with his younger brothers and sisters and remembered with real delight the chaos and fun of being in a big family. I asked him why he did not help Moira more with Stephen. He explained his dilemma. If Moira handed Stephen over to him, the immediate problem was solved, but he felt that Moira seemed very unwilling, either to do this, or to join him in tackling the problem behaviour together. She saw Derek's way of being a parent as indulging Stephen. She saw them as relaxed and happy and herself outside and alone. It was obvious that Derek loved Moira very deeply and wanted to make her happy, but when she asked him to leave her to sort it out and became so angry with him when he intervened, he chose to back off. They began to see how the tension between them had affected their relationship and they genuinely wanted to get closer. It seemed as if Moira throughout her life had become so unused to expecting anyone to help her, that she could not trust anyone, not even Derek, to be on her side. Moira saw it all in terms of a battle and of being on sides. As we talked she warmed to the thought that with Derek's help the situation could improve. She was surprised and delighted when Derek spoke of all the things he loved about her. She had such a low opinion of herself that Derek had given up trying to convince her of all these positive qualities that he valued in her. He had felt quite angry with her for rejecting his love, so that the problem had intensified. Sharing these feelings made it possible to change. Moira began to feel able to ask for and receive loving and understanding support. Derek could show her strategies and ways of coping with Stephen which worked, so that her confidence built up. Instead of Moira and Stephen at daggers drawn, it was Moira and Derek coping together with a rumbustious challenging 3 year old. What about Sharon? The first time I met her she had seemed far too quiet and inhibited. It was as if she was keeping well out of trouble. Not surprising, for she had witnessed the worst of the rows between Moira and Stephen. As the atmosphere in the family eased, so Sharon became more relaxed. Her teacher commented that she seemed more self-confident and had suddenly begun to make progress in reading.

There was something else in Moira's family history that had

profoundly affected her attitude to Stephen refusing food. It was linked to Moira's mother's death at the early age of 52. When I asked about this Moira said, 'The doctor put leukemia on the death certificate, but everyone knew she starved herself to death.' Moira then said that this 'ran in the family', that her mother's mother had also starved herself to death. When Stephen refused food Moira felt the same thing was going to happen again, that it would somehow all turn out to be her fault, so she had to do everything in her power to stop it. When she was trying to ram the food into Stephen's mouth she was, in a sense, desperately trying to keep him from dying. From Stephen's point of view she was assaulting him and he was fighting back. Gradually, over the weeks that we met and talked about all these different aspects of the problem, Moira's anxiety lessened and her attitude to mealtimes became quite relaxed.

When I spoke to Moira some months later she said that Stephen was still a handful but she felt fine and was looking forward to finding some part-time work when he started infants' school.

CHAPTER 5

'But what if there was a witch?'

Why some children are so afraid

Young children inhabit a world of magic, where the line between 'real' and 'imaginary' seems to disappear. The child's fantasy world can be a source of immense joy and creativity in which anything can happen and in which the child reigns supreme. But this imagined world can be inhabited by frightening and disturbing images and feelings which lead to children becoming overwhelmingly terrified. Of course, some children are more easily afraid than others, but all go through phases of seeming frightened by something. It may be the monster who might come up the lavatory, or ghosts in the cupboard. Usually, with understanding and reassurance, parents can help children over these sorts of fears. Sometimes, though, the childhood fears become unmanageable and overwhelming.

Joe was only 3½, although he could have passed for 6. He was a tall, well-built boy with an impressive vocabulary for his age. He came to the clinic with his mother, Mrs Phipps, after he was excluded from playgroup because he repeatedly pushed over other children. Mrs Phipps was puzzled about this behaviour as she had never seen it at home. What worried her more was Joe's anxious preoccupation with witches and ghosts. He would engage her in endless conversations and could not be reassured that his fears were groundless. Here is a fragment of the sort of discussion that would go on by the hour between Joe and his mother.

'Witches *do* steal children don't they, mum?'
'No they don't because there are no such things as witches.'
'But if there was witches they would wouldn't they mum?'
'I wouldn't let anyone hurt you, Joe.'
'If you were asleep they could.'
'They couldn't because they are only in stories. Witches are not real.'
'A witch could take me away on her broomstick and you wouldn't know anything.'
'But Joe, there are no such things as witches.'
'But if there was ... '

It was clear that even with his powerful intellect Joe could not cope with his overwhelming fears.

While Mrs Phipps talked about the worries, Joe painted large swirling patterns full of colour and energy. Mrs Phipps told me that she had had problems in the past but for the first time in her life she was feeling happy and settled. She was therefore even more puzzled that Joe was having worries at that particular time. I asked her about their life together.

Mrs Phipps had married to get away from an unhappy home but her husband had been depressed and increasingly aggressive until, when Joe was about a year, she went back to her parents who took her and Joe in, very grudgingly, and insisted she go out to work full-time. Mrs Phipps felt she had no choice and was very unhappy about her mother looking after Joe. She told me that her mother had 'weird ideas' about bringing up children and though not cruel she was not a warm and loving person. The arrangement lasted about a year until Mrs Phipps found a flat. On her own with Joe she felt very lonely and miserable and went back to work for companionship as much as for the money and Joe went to a childminder. When Joe was 3 Mrs Phipps met and fell in love with Tony, who had left his wife and three children. She planned to move in with Tony within the year and for the first time in her life Mrs Phipps felt deeply contented. She said she had never realised until then what it could feel like to be loved and loving.

Looking back she could see that Joe had had a rough time. Not only were there all the upheavals but she had felt so unhappy and unvalued that she had been unable to give Joe the love and attention that he had needed. As we talked about all the changes in Joe's short life he stopped painting and leaned up against his mother, sucking his thumb. As she held him close she told me, with tears in her eyes, of the difficulty she had had in feeling loving towards Joe. She said that they were just now getting to know each other, as if for the first time. She liked having him around at home. Sometimes he would lie on the floor while she studied or read to herself and he would gaze up at the ceiling or hum quietly and contentedly. At other times he would chatter away, usually about ghosts and witches. After hearing all this I had the feeling that Mrs Phipps would need to do two things to help Joe. She should give up any idea of getting him back to the playgroup, for his apparent poise and intelligence was a cover for the anxious, frightened, baby part of Joe, that made him feel helpless and confused when mixing with so many strange children and adults. Joe and his mother needed time to get to know and trust each other, to enjoy just being together as they would have been when Joe was an infant, if things had been different. Joe could not cope with the big wide world until he felt safe and settled in the most fundamental relationship of all. They had a lot of catching up to do. The second strategy to help Joe was to arrange a number of sessions at the clinic for him and his mother to come and talk about their life together. The witches and ghosts that so frightened Joe were the representations in his imagination of actual people and the mixed feelings that he had had towards them. Even before he was 1 his parents were arguing and fighting, then his father left and there was little contact. Mrs Phipps was depressed and upset and Joe had been cared for by his 'weird' grandmother. Joe could remember that time quite well. Mrs Phipps realised as we explored these memories that sometimes she too had been a 'witch' person to Joe, for in her unhappiness and frustration about the earlier years she had been bad tempered and unloving most of the time. She used to become easily exasperated and lost her temper and shouted and cried when she felt unable to meet Joe's demands. When Joe insisted that 'there might be a witch', he was expressing his fear that the witch mother might reappear. Only time and the good experience of being with a loving mother would reassure Joe that there were no such things as witches.

Joe and his mother enjoyed getting to know each other. Across one summer they did little except please themselves. Joe often lay on the floor like a contented baby, sometimes he would talk baby-talk and often he would climb on to his mother's knee for a cuddle or a story. They walked in the park, fed the ducks and were happy together. Throughout this time Tony was gradually building up his relationship with Joe who had no contact with his own father. It was not easy for Joe to learn to share his mother but he liked Tony, whose caring but firm approach helped Joe to feel safe.

Six months after our first meeting Joe started at nursery school. This time he did not feel that the other children were threatening him so he no longer needed to push them over. He joined in and coped like any other child. A year later Mrs Phipps and Tony were married and Joe started at 'big' school already able to read and enjoy stories which stirred his imagination without overwhelming him.

We can't take her anywhere because she might meet a dog

The Gilberts were really desperate. Their eldest child Janet, aged 9, was terrified of dogs. There was no obvious cause of the fear – she had never been bitten or had a dog jump up on her. Nevertheless, she was rigid with fear whenever she went out lest she see a dog, even a dog on a lead in the distance. There were many places that were now out of bounds for the family because there might be dogs around. Even dogs in books or on television produced an anxious response in Janet. She could no longer visit her best friend because that family had acquired a puppy. She missed out on lots of parties and trips because of her dread. Lots of people, children and adults, are to a greater or lesser extent afraid of dogs and wise to be so, for dogs can sometimes be unpredictable and aggressive. To a small child a dog can seem enormous and forbidding but Janet's fear was so intense that it could be defined as a phobia and it was dominating her and her family's life.

Janet had two younger sisters, Annie, 5, and Clare, 2½. Mr Gilbert was 'something big in the city' and Mrs Gilbert organised the local charity shop. They were a warm, energetic family, involved in numerous activities associated with politics, their children and the golf club. My first meeting with them had had to be rearranged several times due to Mr Gilbert's work commitments, but we all met up in the end. Before I saw the family I already knew that Janet had never had a traumatic experience with a dog, so I knew that I would have to explore with the family what the fear of dogs represented for Janet. During the first meeting I could see that Janet was a very self-controlled, pleasant child who was keen to please but gave little away. Annie was extrovert and attention-seeking in a rather babyish way and by the look, on Janet's face, I guessed that Annie was an irritant in her life. Clare was more like Janet – quiet and gentle, although I heard that she could throw amazingly powerful temper tantrums when she was frustrated. No one in the family could pinpoint the onset of Janet's fear but it had become much more severe over the previous year. I asked if anything significant had been happening to the family and I heard that Mrs Gilbert's mother had made a suicide attempt, and had been admitted to a psychogeriatric unit far away from the Gilberts'. Mrs Gilbert's only brother lived too far away to help so she had to spend a whole day of each weekend visiting her mother, which was always a distressing and sad experience.

Six months previously Annie had her tonsils out after months of severe tonsilitis. Mrs Gilbert recalled Janet's great concern over her sister. The night before Annie's operation Janet had been unable to sleep and Mrs Gilbert found her crying in bed, saying she was afraid Annie would die. Both Mr and Mrs Gilbert were proud that Janet was such a caring and concerned child. Mrs Gilbert said Janet was very like she had been when young, unselfish and helpful. Then she laughed and giving Annie an adoring squeeze said, 'This one is the pest, aren't you darling?' With a little encouragement Janet admitted that she sometimes felt fed up with Annie. I asked her what Annie did that annoyed her and Janet's reply was immediate and very enlightening, 'She is always yapping round my ankles and she makes me cry.' Both parents hearing this jumped in quickly to try and say that Janet did not really mean this, Annie was a handful but she was a sweet child and Janet and she were really good friends and loved each other very much, etc.

After this first meeting it was possible to make some informed guesses about Janet's fear of dogs. She was a 'good girl' who tried to conform to her parents' expectations that she be a responsible and tolerant older sister. She was thoroughly fed up with Annie and had angry and destructive wishes towards her which had caused her to be terrified that Annie might die. Janet was in a conflict between her destructive, angry feelings and her wish to be loving and tolerant. Annie 'yapped' round Janet's ankles and Janet would have liked to yap (or worse) back but could not acknowledge this and so put her own nasty yapping feelings on to dogs, who were then imbued with all the dangerous and retaliatory wishes which really belonged inside Janet. For Janet to be free of her dread of dogs, she would need help in two directions. Firstly, the family and Janet herself would need to acknowledge that she was setting herself too high a standard in being such a good, tolerant and helpful big sister. It seemed as if she was identified with her mother, who had always been unselfish and resilient. For Janet to let herself off the hook Mrs Gilbert might have to reflect on her own needs, which would undoubtedly have an effect on everyone, not least her husband. Even Mrs Gilbert's brother felt the ripples of change in this family, for when Mrs Gilbert acknowledged her resentment at having total responsibility for their ill mother she confronted her brother with this and insisted that he get more involved.

Running parallel with the family's work on being more open

about their feelings, we worked out a plan to help Janet begin to tackle her fear of dogs. Because her terror had been so overwhelming her parents had been loathe to insist she go out, so the plan had to be carefully evolved in graded stages, so that Janet could achieve at each stage, and the success would contribute to a build-up of confidence. The first step was to look at books about dogs, particularly books with pictures of puppies and to watch dogs on television. From this Janet moved on to walking to the post box at the end of the road with her mother, on the understanding that they could cross the road if she saw a dog coming. She was then able to get to the shops and although she continued to be very tense and keyed up she managed each task that was set. When the family went out at weekends, often to the golf course, where there always seemed to be hundreds of dogs, Mr Gilbert promised Janet that if she was afraid he would lift her up to safety and would not put her down until she felt all right. Both parents agreed that the family would not be stopped by Janet's fear from going out and about. If she really felt unable to go with them they would not spend hours, as they had in the past, cajoling and encouraging her, but would simply make other arrangements for her while they were out and would not compensate her for missing out on treats.

Mrs Gilbert took Janet to see some kittens which needed homes, in the hope that the child would like the idea but she became very anxious and could not bring herself to hold one. It was some weeks later that the family went to a cat refuge and it was Janet who asked if they could 'adopt' a large elderly and very dozy cat, whose owner had died leaving the cat homeless. The cat was a great success. Janet became devoted to her and not at all afraid.

Helping Janet over her phobia took many months but gradually she was able to go out with friends and run the risk of meeting dogs. If she went into a house where there was a dog she was able to ask her friend if the dog could be put in another room. She lived with her anxiety, but it no longer dominated her life. Several years later I heard from Mrs Gilbert that Janet had been through quite a 'stroppy time' as a teenager (this sounded healthy) and was through that now and happily settled in a job. 'I wouldn't call her a dog lover, I don't suppose she ever will be, but she leads a full and happy life and that is what we always wanted for her.'

'I am afraid of the end of the world'

That is what 11-year-old Alice Newman would say every bedtime and her parents could not convince her differently, even when they came up with all the scientific arguments that they could muster. Alice found it hard to go to sleep and her normally patient parents would become increasingly exasperated and irritated. Because she was so afraid of going off to sleep Alice was tired nearly all the time. In the evenings she would lie in bed, anxiously watching the sky turn red, certain that this was confirmation of the beginning of the end of the world. Apart from her fears Alice led a full and happy life. She had lots of friends and got on very well at school.

The family's doctor had suggested a mild tranquilliser for Alice to have in the evening but her parents were not happy with this suggestion and wanted to understand the origins of her fears and what they could do to help her, so we had a family meeting with Mr and Mrs Newman, Alice and Edward, who was 8. They had done a lot of hard thinking about Alice's fears but had got nowhere. I asked about recent events in the family and drew a blank. They led an ordered and happy life, no one had been ill, no relatives died, the only important change coming up was that Alice was due to transfer to secondary school the following term, but she seemed very excited and pleased about this. I asked Alice if she could remember when the fear had first come into her mind and her reply was definite and provided a much-needed clue to the puzzle. In the Easter holidays she and Edward had been away for a week with their Sunday school. They had both been very excited about going and had had a thoroughly enjoyable time, but in the middle of the first night Alice had woken suddenly when an aeroplane had gone overhead and she was immediately terrified that the end of the world had come. Part of her knew this was irrational and she felt quite unable to tell anyone about her fear. It was two months before she told her parents and this had taken a lot of courage because she dreaded that they would tell her she was just being silly.

I said to Alice that children and adults who were terrified of something happening to them in the future have often actually had an experience in the past when they were very small, which was so frightening that they spent the rest of their lives with a deep-down dread of it happening again. I wondered if anything had happened to Alice when she was small which might have felt at the time as if the end of her world had come. 'I didn't like it in hospital did I?' Alice said to her parents. 'But you had Nan with you and she really spoiled you,' they said, 'you had a lovely time with her.' Gradually the story unfolded.

When Alice was 2 her father had spent several months in the Far East and for two of these Mrs Newman had joined him while her mother had Alice to stay. Alice had been rather subdued with her Nan, but not difficult or distressed. During her stay at Nan's Alice had developed a serious ear infection and was admitted to hospital for forty-eight hours, partly for observation but also to help Nan, who by now was feeling the sort of panic that anyone experiences when caring for someone else's ill child. Alice's parents arrived back a week later and life quickly got back to normal. The Newmans could not believe that Alice had been upset by what had happened. Alice had few memories of the actual events but she seemed to be in touch with some of the feelings that belonged to that period in her life. With encouragement Alice and her parents talked about that time and Mrs Newman recalled how torn she had felt between staying with Alice or going on a once in a lifetime trip abroad. What had decided her in the end was her own mother's insistence that she should go and her knowledge that Alice would be lovingly and well cared for.

At only 2 years of age Alice had been unable to comprehend what had happened or to have any conception that her parents would return. Her little world had come to an end and her puzzlement and unhappiness and anger had been buried for years, only to burst through when she went away from home again to the camp.

Although Edward had not been around at the time of Alice's trauma, he listened to the story unfolding and made comments on what he heard. He said, 'I am glad you didn't leave *me* behind like that. If you had I would have screamed and screamed.' Everyone laughed and Mr Newman said that Edward always made his feelings clear.

Where the family had previously played down those vital two months, virtually forgetting them, they now had to confront the feelings in all of them. As part of this process Alice went to visit her much loved Nan, to hear her side of events. Although Nan did not really hold with 'all this psychology' she was perfectly willing to talk of the time she had cared for Alice, of her worry when Alice became ill. She even had photos which she had forgotten she had taken from the time when Alice had been with her. Everyone was delighted to see them.

No one could put the clock back, what had happened could not be changed, but instead of trying to forget about it they could talk about it and share the feelings each had of that period in their lives. Alice's familiar world had come to an end for a little while. Now that the adults who loved her could acknowledge and understand the importance to her of what had happened, she could put the panic where it really belonged – in the past – and so she no longer needed to be afraid of the end of the world. Alice could trust her world enough to let go her hold on it and allow herself to fall asleep. Next time she went away without her parents she was not overwhelmed or panic-stricken.

CHAPTER 6

When a habit is more than just a habit

'Lines and Squares'

Whenever I walk in a London Street,
I'm ever so careful to watch my feet;
And I keep in the squares,
And the masses of bears,
Who wait at the corners all ready to eat
The sillies who tread on the lines of the street,
Go back to their lairs,
And I say to them, 'Bears,
Just look how I'm walking in all the squares!'

A. A. Milne, *When We Were Very Young*

A. A. Milne understood so much about the inner world of children and the power of magical thinking. Christopher Robin, as a representative of all young children, could stop the bears from eating him as long as he avoided the lines between the paving stones. The bears in the poem stand for the irrational and rational fears of children. Everyone has their own particular ways of inducing a sense of security. Little habits and routines are woven into normal life so they go unnoticed. Just surviving in modern society is demanding and stressful enough. As well as all the external dangers and threats, there are the emotional ups and downs, the fears and anxieties, excitements and challenges with which everyone has to contend. It is not surprising, therefore, that people develop patterns to their lives which help to give it a structure and meaning, so inducing a feeling of safety and a reduction of anxiety. Young children develop all sorts of odd little habits and rituals. Carrying them out brings a feeling of being in control of their destiny, making sure nothing dreadful happens.

Three children were playing on a garden wall. It was only a low wall so they were quite safe. They were all trying to get to the end without falling off and in the process were having a hilarious time. The first child went along too fast and so kept falling off. The second child was much more careful and when she fell off she climbed back and continued the journey. The third child went along the wall very slowly indeed and only fell off when he was about three steps from the end. He went right back to the beginning and started all over again. The first child lost interest and ran off, shouting to the others to follow. The second finished her walk along the wall and waited for the third, who by this time was making his fourth attempt. She lost patience and as she ran off called to him to jump down and follow her. The third child longed to go with them but felt compelled to complete the walk along the wall. He knew that he would stay there until he succeeded, however long it took. He was not enjoying himself and had by now an anxious, even desperate, look on his face. This little boy had imbued the game with a magical power. He was under a compulsion to complete the task. He could have been thinking and feeling many things. He might have said to himself, 'If I don't do this, something terrible will happen.' This might have been something terrible happening to himself or somebody he loved. It might be less clearly thought out, but just a general dread and overwhelming anxiety that could only be reduced by successful completion of the walk along the wall.

At bedtimes, this little boy had to complete certain rituals. He liked his mother to say 'goodnight' three times in a particular way, then he would say 'goodnight', then she had to kiss him once on each cheek and say 'I love you' each time and he would reply 'I love you too'. Only then would he sleep. Had she refused to carry out this little ritual he would, no doubt, have become distraught and unable to sleep.

Another child had to count the squares in the pavement and when she walked in the park felt compelled to touch each tree trunk three times. If she missed one she would have to run back, however cross her mother became in the meantime. The behaviour of both these children is not in any way unusual. It is only when such rituals, or habits, start to take over a child's life that it is important to try to understand what the underlying anxiety may really be. Why is the child making such frantic attempts to gain some magical control over his world? It may be that his life feels unsafe for all sorts of reasons, some easier to see than others. Upsetting events may have occurred, adults may be quarrelling, or the demands of parents and teachers may be too great. Just as significant are the demands a child makes upon himself in order to be loved and cared for. He feels he must be good and obedient, keep his cross and angry and destructive feelings under control, resist the impulse to say 'no' all the time, or to hit the younger children, to make a mess in the home, or wet his bed – the list of forbidden wishes is endless.

What an effort being 'good'

Beth was 8 years old and had not given up any of the rituals which were rooted in her early childhood. Some of these were lengthy and complex and took up a good deal of her life. If her parents tried to interfere or distract her she became so upset that they had given up trying. Every item in her bedroom had its exact place and woe betide anyone who moved anything. She could not bear to wear a garment that was creased or had even a tiny mark on it. Her bedtime rituals took half an hour, and she always got out of bed a number of times to check that everything in her room was in its place. She was a bright little girl who should have had no difficulty at all with her school work, but she had to have it perfect and could not tolerate making even the tiniest error. She would spend hours over the smallest task and complain that her work was 'no good'. She could not bear to handle clay, or paint, and when she drew a picture all the lines were ruled and measured, with constant rubbings out and corrections, so there was no life or spontaneity in her pictures. She was a very anxious and inhibited little girl. Her brother Greg, 4 years old, was quite a different kettle of fish. Where she was inhibited, he was very outward going. Where she was neat and tidy, he was permanently in a mess. Where she was anxious, he was confident. Mr and Mrs Hicks felt that Beth's problems went back a long way. She was a much wanted baby, born after Mrs Hicks had had three miscarriages and had nearly given up hope of ever having a baby. Both parents were thrilled when Beth was born and Mrs Hicks was determined to be a full-time mother. She was 38 when Beth was born and was taken by surprise at how exhausted she felt in those early months. She had always been very capable in all aspects of her life, and admitted that she was a bit of a perfectionist. After Beth was born she could not compromise her standards, neither could she allow herself to lean more on her husband, who was quite unaware at that time of the enormous strain on Mrs Hicks of keeping up appearances. When Beth was just one Mrs Hicks became pregnant again but miscarried at three months. Neither she nor her husband allowed themselves to mourn the loss of this baby, preferring to get back into the swing of life and accept that Beth was to be their only child. Mrs Hicks recalled that even before this pregnancy Beth was already clean and dry in the day but when Mrs Hicks came out of hospital Beth, not surprisingly, reverted to wetting herself, although only for a few days. As we all talked of this unhappy episode in the family's life both Mr and Mrs Hicks got in touch with the sad feelings which they had earlier denied and pushed under, while they got on with their lives. Beth, though so very young at the time, seemed to have sensed her mother's underlying sadness, in the face of which Beth had controlled her own wishes to demand her mother's attention, to cry, have temper tantrums or lose control by wetting herself.

When Mrs Hicks became pregnant with Greg she did everything she could to prevent another miscarriage. She rested as much as possible and recalled that Beth was particularly good at this time, making few demands on her and playing on her own for quite long periods. Then Greg was born and both parents were relieved and overjoyed. By now Beth was already a self-controlled and 'good' little girl. She gave no clues that she was in any way put out by Greg's arrival. Her parents recalled that Beth did not seem to enjoy being with Greg. Most children take great delight in watching and helping with a baby and when the baby crawls and responds and interacts with them they have increasing pleasure in the relationship. Where most children would thoroughly enjoy seeing a baby trying to feed itself and getting food all round its face and on the floor, Beth was disgusted. She couldn't bear to see a dirty nappy or be near Greg when he was sick or dribbled. When he cried she became anxious and would leave the room. Her rituals were by now very lengthy and complicated and were affecting everyone in the family. It was at this time that the family sought help.

As the story unfolded in the family meeting we began to understand how these obsessional rituals had been Beth's attempt to keep control of her forbidden impulses. All her liveliness and strong feelings had been pushed down and she had become inhibited and overcontrolled. During the first few family meetings Beth was tense and withdrawn and seemed to be struggling to control her wish to carry out some of her touching and counting rituals. When she began to see and hear that her parents could be open with their opinions and feelings, this gave her the confidence to risk letting down some of her defences. One day, before they arrived, I had put out a box of brand new plasticine. A few minutes into the session Beth tentatively leaned forward and took a piece. At first she very carefully made a number of identical squares. Then Greg moved over and joined her and in his uninhibited way began to roll out long snakes of plasticine on the table top, which he then banged with a wooden hammer. Having watched him for a few minutes, Beth joined in. She rolled out the snakes and gave them to Greg to hit. They both got thoroughly involved in the excitement of the game and Beth began to be more lively and stopped glancing anxiously towards her parents.

In the next session the two children were sorting out a large and very untidy dolls' house, which was in the room. Greg found the bathroom suite, which included a miniature lavatory, complete with a lid. He chortled with delight, while Beth watched his every move with a mixture of fascination and embarrassment. It was obvious that she was longing to join in what she perceived as a 'naughty' or 'dirty' game. Her mother sensed that Beth needed permission to join in the play, so she herself showed interest in the bathroom suite and commented what a nice loo it was and how they could do with a new one at home. A few minutes later Beth uncovered a toy potty. She was obviously delighted and she and Greg proceeded to put the tiny baby dolls on the potty one by one. The performance that followed was an eye-opener. Their play became more and more excitable. The potty was spilt and a mummy doll was brought in to spank the baby. Beth was taking on the part of both mummy and baby. Baby doll was violently smacked and even jumped on by the mother doll, while the baby, far from becoming obedient and good after such treatment, shouted and screamed back, insisting that she would do poos and wees on the floor. It was the first of a series of playlets, spontaneously created by Beth and Greg, in which Beth could give expression to many deeply repressed wishes and longings. Her parents reported that the uninhibited games were continuing at home and they could see that Beth was relaxing and enjoying life more. She was much noisier and more argumentative, and though often rather babyish, her parents understood that she had some catching up to do. Through her play and her growing understanding that her parents did not disapprove, Beth was able to give up her obsessional rituals. An important factor in bringing about this change was her parents' acknowledgement of their sadness and the strain of keeping up a front. Although this meant facing a certain amount of pain, it led to them being much more accepting of

themselves and each other and freer therefore to join in with the
playfulness of their children.

Sexual anxiety and obsessional rituals

Kevin Armstrong kept his obsessional rituals a secret. Everyone knew
him to be a shy, quiet 14 year old. Even his mother and stepfather
had no idea of the complexity of the rituals that he had developed.
One night when the family had gone to bed Mrs Armstrong found
Kevin downstairs checking that all the doors were locked. She sent
him back to bed, but then at 3 am she found him downstairs again,
checking all the locks. When she told him there was no need for him
to worry, that she and dad had locked up he broke down and cried,
and revealed that this was only one of many rituals and obsessions
that he had to carry out each day and he was terrified that he was
going mad. Mrs Armstrong arranged for an appointment for Kevin
to see the family doctor, who referred him to the clinic.

Kevin was one of a large family. His 19-year-old sister was
married, living a few miles away. His 17-year-old sister lived at
home and had a full-time job. Kevin shared a bedroom with his 11-
year-old brother. Kevin's parents had divorced when he was 5. His
mother had remarried when he was 11 and a year later had identical
twin boys, now 3, who not surprisingly were a central focus of the
family's life.

The first family meeting gave a number of clues as to why Kevin
might be emotionally upset. When the family sat down Kevin
positioned himself between his mother and stepfather. Then when I
asked what everyone called Mr Armstrong the older girls said that
they called him Mick. The 11 year old called him dad, but Kevin said
he didn't call him anything, which felt to me as if Kevin was not
accepting Mr Armstrong as a member of the family. Kevin looked
very different from the rest of the family. His mother said he was the
spitting image of his own father, John, and then she added quickly

that she meant only in looks, not in nature. There was a silence after she said this in which Kevin looked anxious and uncomfortable. Mrs Armstrong hinted that her first marriage had been problematic and that John had what she called 'personal problems' which led to the breakdown in their relationship. The girls had kept in touch with him, and saw him occasionally, but neither of the boys wanted contact with him and he had shown no interest in them.

Kevin's sister had been aware of some of his habits and on occasions had teased him, in a mild sort of way, about being 'Mr Clean', for he washed his hands frequently and spent hours in the bathroom morning and night. Everyone had noticed how tense and jumpy Kevin had become and also mentioned how fussy he was over his food, preferring to prepare his own and refusing to handle other people's dishes or cutlery. Kevin had constant battles with his younger brother over their shared room. He needed everything to be neat and tidy and in its place, and could not tolerate it when his brother's possessions encroached on his territory.

The picture that was building up was of an adolescent boy desperately trying to keep under control impulses which he felt were forbidden and dangerous. He was trying to wash away his guilt and seemed afraid that his badness would affect those closest to him. He was well aware that his compulsions were irrational and was afraid that he was going mad. I thought it likely that Kevin had great anxieties about his developing sexual impulses and that this was at some level linked to his early life experiences, as well as his feelings about his parents and stepfather. As we were going to have to talk about sex, I suggested that the next meeting should be without the twins.

I wondered how much the family knew of the reasons for their mother's divorce. Mrs Armstrong hinted that her present husband and the girls knew quite a lot of what had gone wrong, but she had not felt it right to tell the boys. As the session went on Kevin began to talk of his memories of his father and he shocked his mother by vividly recalling rows between his parents at night. Their bedroom had been next to his and he had heard his mother refusing to have sex and accusing his father of having only one thing on his mind and of disgusting her. At the time Kevin had been completely confused by what he overheard. He recalled his father as a kind and gentle person, and had some very happy memories of him, but then there was this other father, the one who his mother shouted at and was disgusted by, and in the end had asked to leave. Although Kevin had been very young he had already formed the impression that something was going on in his parents' bed which was disgusting and frightening and caused his mother to be angry and upset.

No one had been aware of how much Kevin missed his father. In his imagination Kevin felt very identified with his own father. Everyone said he was just like him and he was intensely jealous and hurt when Mick came on the scene and made Kevin's mother really happy. Then to add insult to injury, the twins were born and received so much love and attention.

I encouraged the family to share their experiences of growing up. The girls made it clear that they had always been able to talk to their mum about everything and anything. If they had worries about growing up, boyfriends and sex, they could talk to each other and to her. Mick seemed an easy, open, sort of person and told me of his willingness to talk about 'the birds and the bees' with Kevin but he had always felt that Kevin froze him out and did not want to talk to him.

So here was Kevin, a boy well into adolescence, who in the normal course of events would be having sexual fantasies and longings and the urge to masturbate, but who was identified with a father whose sexuality had been repulsive to mum and who had in the end been rejected. He could not turn to Mick to help him with his worries over sex because he had not acknowledged his jealousy of Mick, who had confidently established himself as mum's sexual partner. In Kevin's eyes the twin boys were a confirmation of Mick's powers as a potent man, who could cause the birth of not one but two male children! It was very important for Kevin to hear from his mother a more balanced view of her first marriage. Of course, it would not have been appropriate for her to have been too open about the details of their sexual difficulties, but she was able to fill in lots of gaps in Kevin's understanding. She explained how happy they had been for several years, but then there had been a gradual growing apart and increased tension between them. At one stage Kevin's father had an affair, which had led to a number of painful and emotional scenes, some of which it was now clear, Kevin had overheard and badly misunderstood. Kevin was greatly relieved to hear about the good things there had been in that marriage and was also helped by his mother's acknowledgement that the difficulties had been as much hers as her first husband's.

The next step was for Kevin to have help with his anxiety and guilt over his sexual longings. His sisters had their mother to help them, the younger boy said he knew all about 'all that' from his mates, but Kevin had no close friends and no ongoing relationship with his father. Mick was the obvious person to help Kevin and he undertook to have 'a chat or two' with Kevin. It felt easier for Mick now so many feelings had been aired and he was genuinely very sad for Kevin that such a normal stage in his life should have become such a burden. Mick was no longer prepared to be frozen out by Kevin. He knew that the boy needed him and he was determined to be of help.

Over the following weeks Mick and Kevin had some man to man chats. Mick told Kevin about his own adolescence and how he had learned about sex and of some of the muddles and anxieties he had had as a teenager. He talked to him about wet dreams and masturbation, and about getting on with girls. He also told Kevin that he could understand that Kevin had felt confused and unhappy and jealous, but most important of all, he told Kevin how much he liked him.

Gradually Kevin gave up his obsessional habits and began to relax and enjoy family life. Now that he no longer had to feel guilty about his sexuality, he did not have to fear contaminating his family. When I met him with Mr and Mrs Armstrong several months' later, he told me he had started going to discos and had made some friends. His mother told me that Kevin was now the scruffiest member of the family and only remembered to wash if he was going out with his friends – a far cry from the compulsive 'Mr Clean' that I had first met.

Kevin had also been to see his own father a couple of times and they liked each other. Kevin laughed telling me that he had felt very shy and not known what to say, and then he realised his father felt just the same and they had been able to talk about it.

Kevin had needed to do a lot of work, sorting out the muddles in the past and the present. As he felt less bad about himself, and particularly about his sexuality he was freed up to make friends, increase his confidence and move in a more healthy way towards becoming an adult.

CHAPTER 7

A child is being killed

Nightmare or truth?

By the time parents seek professional help for their child or family the problem may have been around for quite a while. There is always the understandable hope that the worry will simply disappear with time, which is often the case. If it persists parents will probably try all sorts of ways of tackling the problem, depending on its nature and severity, before feeling justified in asking for outside help. Some emotional upsets appear to erupt so suddenly and incomprehensibly that parents feel understandably alarmed and need help urgently. Grappling with the problem at the moment of crisis is usually much more productive than hours spent looking at worries which seem, at least temporarily, to have gone off the boil.

Mr and Mrs Williams lived with Mrs Williams' children, Ian, 12 and Sarah, 8, in a village with no by-pass. Huge lorries would thunder through night and day and their front door was almost in the road. Hardly surprising then that they were terrified of Sarah getting killed when, night after night, she would wake screaming and rush through the house as if to escape from something or someone horrifying.

This had all started suddenly about two weeks before Mrs Williams telephoned me. She said that at some time every night Sarah would either dash round looking awake but apparently asleep, or she would get up, again in her sleep, gather up her clothes, toys and anything else she could lay her hands on, taking all these things to bed as if she were hiding from someone. One night she even took her large waste-paper basket under her duvet. Her screams were ear-piercing and Mrs Williams was quite worried about what the neighbours might be thinking. Sarah had no memory of all this night-time drama and Mrs Williams could think of no reason for the sudden onset of such disturbed behaviour. I was able to meet the family the following day.

I had arranged the room with a table in the middle on which were large sheets of paper and lots of coloured pencils. As soon as the family came in Sarah settled down to draw, while Ian could not quite decide whether to join her or to have a large armchair. In the end he too decided to draw. I noticed that both children referred to Mr Williams as 'dad' and that the family brought into the room with them a warm and caring atmosphere. I listened to the detail of the night terrors and was convinced that Sarah had no memory of them and that she was as puzzled as the rest of the family about what was going on. Not surprisingly she also looked rather tired and Mrs Williams was concerned that Sarah was not getting proper sleep. Indeed, the whole family were exhausted as they were all awake, sometimes for several hours.

When a child suddenly produces disturbed behaviour the cause is often easy to understand – sudden illness, or a death in the family, the disappearance for whatever reason of a parent, starting a new school – so many life events are anxiety-provoking and may lead to a brief period of upset in the child. But the Williams could think of nothing significant. The only slight worry that Sarah had had recently concerned her school, which for one term had been without a head teacher and left all the other members of staff under a good deal of strain and the morale in school at that time was quite low. Sarah enjoyed going to school but was often found day-dreaming and not getting on with her work. She had been a little upset recently when her teacher had smacked a couple of boys who had been very difficult. She had come home and told her mother and said that she hoped her teacher would never smack her.

While we talked Sarah had been producing an imaginative colour drawing of a stripy tiger and a camel with two people riding on it. I asked Sarah who they were. A fleeting worried look came over Sarah's face. She looked at her mother as if afraid of revealing something forbidden. Mrs Williams encouraged her to say whatever she wanted, and Sarah then told me it was a picture of herself and Ian at the zoo. I asked when they had been to the zoo and after a second of hesitation she said, 'We went with Adrian a long time ago.' Mrs Williams was astonished and went on to explain that the last time the children had seen their real father, Adrian, he had taken them to the zoo, but this was at least two years previously.

This is a wonderful example of how children, through their drawing or play will draw attention to their worries and problems. It seemed clear that Sarah was introducing Adrian, bringing him into the session, but also that she had been worried about doing this through her loyalty to Mr Williams, whom she saw as her dad. The story unfolded and as the family talked Sarah took another sheet of paper and began to draw and write. I heard a little about Mrs Williams' first marriage to Adrian, of how unhappy they were and of his increasing violence towards her. Looking back she could not imagine why she stayed so long, but at the time she had felt there was nowhere to go. They were very hard up and living in bad accommodation in the country, far from any town. She had not been able to tell her parents what was going on. She described her mother as a chronic worrier and her parents had never approved of Adrian, whom she had only married to get away from her unhappy home. Ian remembered his father's violence and how, when he was only 6, he had run several hundred yards up the road to try and telephone the police. He told me how terrified he had been and of his frequent attempts to protect his mother.

All the time they talked Sarah drew and wrote until the paper was covered in what looked like a story from a comic, little stick figures with words and balloons. In the middle she had written 'I love you', and then crossed it out and put 'I hate you'. She had done this several times. The drawings were all full of action, with people falling over, while others were saying 'Oh, no, what is the matter, what is happening, oh no, oh no'. It all looked very alarming indeed. I asked Sarah what was happening to those people in her drawing. She said they were being hurt and falling over and in the bottom picture someone was falling on to a fire and getting burnt. Then Mrs Williams spoke of the events which finally led to her decision to take both children and leave Adrian. On one terrible evening he had tried to hit her. Ian had rushed to get help and Sarah who was only 3 had accidentally got in her father's way and he had pushed her so she fell with her face against an electric fire. She would have the scar on her cheek all her life. As Mrs Williams spoke Ian joined in to say how terrified he had been, but Sarah sat listening, quite still, gazing at her mother as if she were hearing the story for the first time. Then Ian said, 'It was all like a sort of nightmare but it is all over now and we are all happy again.' I said that for Ian it was like a nightmare but one which he knew had really happened, but perhaps Sarah could not remember it when she was awake, only when she was asleep, so for her it was a real nightmare. I thought it would be helpful to talk it over a bit more, so that Sarah could begin to sort out what was real and what was imagined. It was understandable that Mr and Mrs Williams should not have dwelt on the awful past, but put all their efforts into building their new happier life. They had taken the view that it was all best forgotten, but they could see as we talked that it was the muddled memories that were at the bottom of Sarah's night terrors.

In normal circumstances, little girls from around 3 years of age love their fathers with special intensity. Sarah must have been in a terrible conflict at that time, for she may have both loved and feared Adrian. Even though the last visit from him had been two years earlier it seemed quite possible that she might still think about him and wonder what he was doing. I put some of this into words and Sarah listened and nodded. Then she got up and sat herself comfortably on Mr Williams' knee, showing me that he was the 'dad' she really loved and who cared for her. Ian said he sometimes thought about Adrian and wondered if he would ever try to steal his children back. He said it had been strange when they went out with him to the zoo. He was really nice all day. It seemed then that Ian was in touch with his sadness that Adrian had not been able to be like that all the time. He quite surprised his mother by telling her of his anxiety that Adrian might come looking for him. Sometimes when he came out of school he would peer anxiously up the road, almost as if he expected his father to be there. It was as if under the real fear there lingered some hidden longing to know his father and to be near him. It is often very surprising to adults to realise that children can hold on to good feelings for a parent who has treated them very badly or abandoned them.

Together we had reached some real understanding about Sarah's recent upset but why had it all erupted then and not years before? It often seems to be the case that frightening, sad or painful experiences get forgotten, pushed down into the unconscious. Although the actual memories may be lost, the feelings about the early events can linger on and may surface much later in life if something happens to reawaken them. In Sarah's case it was the unexpected and alarming angry outburst from her usually calm teacher which seems to have been the trigger to her problem. For when the teacher slapped the boys it reawakened in Sarah the feelings of fear and panic associated with her early life and led to the night terrors which, after just two exploratory meetings with the family, had ceased as quickly as they had begun.

I am not suggesting that we go on and on about past events. That would be burdensome and boring, to say the least. But we must acknowledge that children get easily confused between memory and imagination. In order to recover from the effects of trauma and emotional pain, especially when it occurs very early in life, a child needs to be told the truth about those events, so that gradually the past can be put behind and not interfere in the way of future relationships and life events.

Sarah's story illustrates another problem which can arise when one parent is seen as the bad one. In Mrs Williams' eyes Adrian was the bad one and neither Ian nor Sarah felt comfortable even mentioning his name. In spite of all the fear, it seemed clear that those children had held on to some good feelings for Adrian. Mr and Mrs Williams were able to acknowledge and allow this to be so, which seemed to surprise and relieve the children. Everyone in the family had been protecting each other from getting upset by trying to 'forget' the past. Sarah's crisis had reminded them all of the pain and fear they had lived through which could not be forgotten. After these memories were shared and the muddled feelings faced, the family could look forward to their life together.

In the third and last meeting Sarah drew a beautiful cottage set in rolling hills. Roses grew up the walls and a bright sun shone optimistically in the blue sky. They were moving away to start a life in the countryside. I never heard from them again but I believe that Sarah continued to sleep peacefully.

CHAPTER 8

'I wish I had died in that aeroplane crash'

Depression in an 8 year old

Feeling unhappy and being depressed are quite different. This is true for adults and it is just as true for children. A sad child can be comforted and consoled, a depressed child is cut off from the consolation and unable to make use of the attention and love that caring adults may offer. Parents of a depressed child feel helpless and guilty that nothing they do seems to make their child happy. They may then become angry and guilty about being angry. The child, sensing the parents' upset, becomes more withdrawn and so more miserable and depressed. Everyone in the family needs rescuing from this vicious circle.

Colin lived with his parents Mr and Mrs Clark and his sister Mandy, who was 6. One sunny afternoon Mrs Clark saw Colin sitting on a step in the garden. She thought he looked bored and suggested he help her tidy a cupboard in the kitchen. To her amazement, Colin burst into tears and angrily replied that she always asked him to do everything, it wasn't fair and he wished he was dead. She tried to calm him down but he rushed from the room and went upstairs slamming his bedroom door. This sort of outburst was so completely out of character for Colin that Mrs Clark thought he might be overtired or sickening for an illness. She told her husband what had happened and he went up to talk to Colin. Mr

Clark was a kind and caring father who could not bear arguments or unhappiness. He pointed out to Colin that his mother had only been trying to interest him in something and that it was silly and upsetting to everyone to talk of wanting to be dead. He encouraged Colin out of his room and all agreed to 'forget' the incident. Colin became his usual self, quite quiet and co-operative. A few days later there happened to be a news item on the television about an aeroplane crash, in which everyone had been killed. Colin watched intently but said nothing. Later on, when his mother went to say goodnight, she found him in tears. He could not tell her what was wrong but said that he wished he had died in the aeroplane crash. She was shocked and frightened but did not tell her husband because of her anxiety about burdening him with worries. She hoped a good night's sleep would do the trick and that Colin would forget what he had said and felt.

A week after this incident, Mrs Clark was tidying Colin's bedroom. She picked up his pillow and there, underneath it, was a bottle of pills which he had taken from the bathroom cupboard. He would have to have moved a chair to stand on in order to reach this cupboard, which was high up on the wall, and although the pills he had taken were in fact not particularly dangerous Mrs Clark was now really frightened. It was at this point in the story that she contacted the clinic and I arranged to meet the family.

They were a strikingly attractive family who at first sight could have walked straight off an advertisement for breakfast cereal. Mandy was clearly delighted to find paper and crayons ready on the table. She began to draw enthusiastically. I saw the warm and proud look in her parents' eyes. Colin sat quietly and ignored the plasticine near him on the table. Gradually I heard the events which had led up to this meeting. When Mrs Clark was telling me of Colin's wish to be dead she stressed that of course he did not really mean it. Perhaps it was just to get attention. My own feeling, which I put into words, was that it certainly had got Colin some attention but maybe he really did mean it too, and if so, we needed to understand why Colin wanted to be dead. Maybe there were some feelings that were difficult to talk about but it might be helpful to try. I handed round the plasticine and we all rolled it and made models while we talked. I heard about and saw for myself how different the children were in their characters. Mandy was confident and rather bossy, she had lots of friends and was involved in out-of-school activities. She and Colin played quite well but she tended to beat him at games of skill and speed. When I asked Colin how this made him feel, he shrugged his shoulders and said he did not mind. I asked if they argued and all agreed they did sometimes, but that Colin was 'good' about that and usually Mandy got her own way. Colin said this was right, and went on to say that Mandy got more of everything than he did, it wasn't fair. Both his parents rushed in to say this was not the case, they treated the children just the same, but Colin never seemed satisfied, he was always comparing what he had with what Mandy had and making a case for being hard done by or deprived. His parents tried and tried to satisfy him but never succeeded. I said it sounded as if Colin needed a lot of proof that his parents loved him. Then he began to cry and through his tears blurted out that that was why he wanted to be dead, to make them love him. Colin obviously needed comforting at this stage but neither parent moved towards him so I said maybe Colin would like a cuddle. His mother looked sad as she told me that he never wanted a cuddle from her, so she had given up trying. Mr Clark got a handkerchief out and patted Colin on the shoulder while telling him to 'cheer up son'.

As our time was nearly up' we looked at what everyone had made from the bits of plasticine. Mr Clark had made a steam engine – it turned out that he was building one in the garden shed, but he said Colin was not interested in it and anyway it would be dangerous for him to mess about with all the tools. Mrs Clark had made a basket with coloured eggs in. Mandy had made a large hippopotamus with a wide open mouth while Colin had made a very small curled up hedgehog which he had carefully marked with his nails to show the prickles. This hedgehog was Colin, small and turned in on himself for protection with his spines ready to prick, particularly if the hippo came near. Colin had made his dilemma clear. He was full of jealousy and anger and he did not know what to do with these feelings, so he held them in, turned his rage on to himself and became quite suicidal. He made it difficult for his parents to rescue him as he hid his real feelings under an apparently calm and generally co-operative personality. All their attempts to prove they loved him as much as Mandy had failed. He was making them feel hopeless and angry. Colin's passivity in the face of Mandy's demanding and controlling behaviour was quite a serious problem, because I sensed that arguments and fights between the children would not be welcome by these parents. I also wondered about Mr Clark's reluctance to encourage Colin to help with the steam engine and why had Mrs Clark accepted Colin's rejection of her and not fought her way back to rescue him. Understanding how it had come about was one thing, but the most important thing at this stage was that Colin's parents had taken his cry for help seriously, and it seemed unlikely that he would now need to threaten suicide in order to draw attention to his distress.

At our next meeting I brought out the plasticine models to remind us all of where we left off last time. I said I wondered if Colin could tell what would happen if the hedgehog unrolled. He smiled at this and said it would run around sticking prickles into everyone. What would they all do then I wondered? 'Stamp on him,' was the reply. I asked how the family would feel if Colin was more assertive and let some of his cross prickly feelings come out. Mandy laughed and said that she would hit him if he hit her. Much to her and his parents' surprise Colin said quite firmly that he would hit her back. Mr Clark then intervened to say that Colin knew that boys should not hit their sisters. Before Colin could react, Mrs Clark turned to her husband and said that she had always felt it wrong that they had told Colin not to hit back. Mr Clark replied that he did not want Colin to be a bully and that it was much better to work out a peaceful solution to conflict. I asked Mr Clark how he had coped with bullies and he said he had never been able to protect himself from other boys' teasing. His brother had made his life a misery by his cruel taunts and physical attacks, against which Mr Clark had felt helpless. He had hidden himself away as much as possible throughout his childhood and often felt very unhappy and had not known how to tell anyone. Mrs Clark was one of four children and well used to rivalries and fights as well as the warmth and fun of family life. She had longed to encourage Colin to stand up for himself but did not want to undermine her husband, who was an anxious, worrying man.

This conversation threw some light on Mr Clark's reluctance to let his son into the work shed, for as we talked further it became clear that Mr Clark did not believe that Colin wanted to be with him so his invitations to Colin were given in a half-hearted way, the result being that Colin did not believe that his father really wanted his company. We did some work around this whole question which ended up with both Colin and his father being pleased at the thought that they wanted each other and would share an activity.

The other big problem for these parents was their failure to satisfy Colin. They were scrupulous about trying to be fair, even buying one child a gift on the other one's birthday to avoid jealousy, but Mandy was always pleased with whatever she got, while Colin was always dissatisfied. This led both parents to feel as if they were failing Colin and the resulting guilt drove them on to try even harder to make Colin happy, to prove they loved him. It was impossible for either parent to admit how cross they felt. They could not feel safe with their anger so they constantly covered it up. For Colin to feel loved in a real way he needed his parents to feel safe to say 'no' and to stop trying to prove their love with gifts. If they could learn to admit their angry and irritated feelings then Colin would feel better about owning those feelings himself and not have to bottle them up.

It was becoming clear that it was Mr Clark and not Colin who was the most vulnerable member of the family. His self-esteem was low and he easily became anxious and withdrawn. Nevertheless, he was prepared to look at these problems and Mrs Clark was relieved to have permission to be more open with her feelings and not need to protect her husband from them. Mandy, who had previously had exclusive rights to confidence and cheerfulness in the family, had to adjust to her brother's increasing assertiveness. He began to stand up for himself and she learned that not everything was going her way. Although initially she was a bit upset about this, it was clearly a much better preparation for life. Mr Clark began to believe in Colin's need for him and this made both of them much happier. Both the parents learned that there is no such thing as being completely fair with children. They stopped letting themselves feel guilty if Colin compared himself unfavourably with Mandy. Colin felt safe enough to give up being so compliant. In some ways he was more difficult, but not nearly as worrying. There was more life in the house. More noise too and arguments, but also a lot more fun. Everyone felt freer and the depression that Colin had been carrying lifted.

CHAPTER 9

'I will always love my lovable mum'

John's attempt to cope with his mother's death

Helping children to accept the reality of death is one of the greatest challenges faced by parents. It touches on all the deepest fears and uncertainties that are part of human existence. All those impossible and unanswerable questions about where dead people go – what does it mean to be dead? – does it hurt? – will I die? – will you die? – where is heaven? These direct questions may simply be the child's natural quest for knowledge about the real world and as such can be dealt with in a matter-of-fact way – including the admission that some of the questions cannot be answered. Those anxious questionings about death may be the child's way of sharing a dread of aloneness and separation from familiar and loved adults, and are likely to be a reflection of the child's current life fears to do with separation anxiety rather than about death itself.

In the normal course of life children build up experiences which gradually prepare them to cope with the death of those they love. Many very young children become passionately attached to a particular toy or a piece of blanket, or some other small object which becomes imbued or invested by the child with the longing, loving feelings he has for his mother – the object serves as a stand-in for the mother and will induce a sense of safety and comfort in the child, whenever he needs it. If this security blanket (as Linus in the Peanuts cartoon calls it) is lost or removed before the child is ready to do without it, he will be inconsolable and likely to react in ways which are similar to an adult grief reaction. First comes the frantic search for the lost object, followed by the rage at not finding it during which the small child may refuse to be comforted. Then, if the parent is available and sympathetic the child will, through his crying, give expression to his sadness about the loss of the longed for object and reach a stage of acceptance from which he can recover and move on in his emotional development. If parents, for whatever reason, ignore the child's distress or forbid it, these unexpressed and unresolved feelings may stay with the child who senses that it is dangerous to show emotions and is therefore less well equipped to cope with future loss and bereavement.

In the normal course of family life a child's first experience of death is likely to be when a grandparent dies. Most children can cope with the idea that elderly people are tired and ready to die. Although they miss the person and feel sad that he or she is no longer there, they recover very quickly and get on with their lives. Problems may arise if the child is caught up in the parents' difficulty in coping with their own loss. Some parents feel it will harm their children to see their parents weeping and not coping well with life. Children get excluded from family discussions about an imminent or actual death, and not allowed to attend funerals because parents do not want them to be upset or witness their parents' distress. This deprives children of a chance to learn through sharing with others, that tears, sadness and death are as much part of life as laughter, joy and birth. If they are kept out of the family's shared grief children may be left with all sorts of confused feelings and fears, not least that they are in some way responsible for their parents' distress. They will be deprived of an opportunity for emotional growth without which they will be ill-equipped to cope with the losses which are an inevitable part of adult life.

For some children the experience of death is sudden and

devastating and the effects far-reaching. This is the story of just one little boy who was faced with the unexpected death of his mother, and of the implications of that tragedy on his subsequent life.

John was 12 when his father, Alan, and stepmother, Maggie, asked for help with John who refused to communicate with Maggie or her two daughters, Alison, 14, and Susan, 10. This had been going on since Alan and Maggie's marriage two years previously, but a crisis point had been reached when Maggie discovered that John had taken some underwear from Alison's drawer and hidden it in his bed. Maggie had confronted John over this and he did not deny it. Maggie had reached the end of her tether and insisted that Alan 'get something done' about John. She did not want her daughters involved lest they get upset and worried so my colleague, Nick, and I agreed to see them on their own without any of the children. At that time Maggie openly expressed her feeling that she could not go on with John being so difficult, while Alan was terrified that the new marriage was under serious threat. They were obviously concerned about the sexual implications of John's taking of the underwear.

They described how John would refuse to respond to anyone but Alan. He would pretend not to hear, ignore requests to do this or that, and when he reached the point of having to hear he would make even the slightest demand seem like a great burden. John continued to talk to his father, but all Alan's attempts to get John to open up with his stepmother and stepsisters failed. If Maggie, Alison or Susan accidentally touched John as they walked past he would flinch, and if they sat near him on the sofa he would turn his back. We heard that Susan was the only one who took no notice of his behaviour and carried on talking and bumping into John in her usual extrovert way.

We asked about John's mother, Jill, and the circumstances of her death when John was only 8. Alan told us that Jill was a quiet rather shy person who enjoyed being at home. John had a very normal early life and had always been a quiet, self-contained little boy who preferred to be at home amusing himself and being with Jill. He had few friends but went happily to school. Alan was always a sociable person involved in a number of clubs and societies as well as working hard in his small business. One day when Jill was only 35 she had a stroke and was rushed to hospital. That afternoon on his way home from school a neighbour's child told John that his mother was dead.

Alan's mother immediately came to stay with them. John did not go to the funeral because Alan did not want to upset him. Alan and Granny did all they could to protect John from pain. After Granny went home Alan arranged for a kind woman to be in the house every day when John returned from school. Alan kept his grief under control but could remember little of how John had been during that time. He told us that John had always been a quiet, introverted child and just 'got on with life'. Alan recalled happy times with John when they had gone on holiday together or taken trips to museums and castles. Alan described John's life after his mother's death as rather solitary and empty but they both survived.

Then Alan met Maggie who had divorced her violent alcoholic husband and was successfully rebuilding her life with her two daughters. Both Alan and Maggie were determined to put the children's needs before their own and thought long and hard before marrying. Alan recalled that John was non-committal about what he felt and Alan assumed, as well he might, that in a family with a new mother John would begin to come alive again. Alan and Maggie knew the settling down period would be difficult but were determined to make it work for them all. Maggie was a bright, capable and forceful woman who had been brought up to believe that life was for living and nothing was gained by harking back to the past. She was prepared to be understanding of the children's needs but expected them to make an effort to create a good feeling in the new family. Her girls were flourishing. They liked Alan and were relaxed and happy in that relationship. John was the problem.

When Alan and Maggie married they lived in Alan's home and Maggie recalled how John had prepared his parents' bedroom with everything in place as his mother had had it. Maggie changed it round as she wanted it and put a few of Jill's possessions in a box for

John and then put her own things in place. All this happened in Wales. After a year the family moved to their new home near London, to a house so small they were almost tripping over each other. The children had to make the move into the local comprehensive school – quite a different environment from the small Welsh-speaking schools they had previously attended – money was short and tension was high. Then John took the underwear and that was the final straw. Alan and Maggie agreed to bring the whole family for a meeting with the two of us. We all agreed not to mention the underwear incident at this stage. Neither of the girls knew what had happened and clearly it would have been very difficult for John if the matter came up at the first meeting.

The children were just as they had been described. Alison and Susan were attractive, alert girls, genuinely concerned about John's refusal to join in the family. They spoke of their pleasure in having Alan as a 'dad', the fun they had playing rough-houses with him and their happiness at having a 'real' family again. John sat silently while they chattered on, and when I commented that it must be quite difficult sharing a dad whom he had had all to himself he nodded agreement and looked sadly at the floor. At this stage Nick and I had no idea what the children called the parents – but I had a sense that this might be a problem and indeed this soon emerged to be the case. The girls had no difficulty calling Alan 'dad', for neither had any memory of their own natural father and so were really pleased to have a dad at last. Alan and Maggie were so keen to make this new family a real family they expected all three children to call them 'mum' and 'dad'. We sensed that John could not call Maggie 'mum' without feeling disloyal to his own mother and we said so. Again John nodded his agreement and a sad feeling came into the room. We suggested to Alan and Maggie that they might need to help John find another name for Maggie, and she responded immediately by saying she did not mind what John called her and he could decide.

We encouraged Alan to talk in this meeting about Jill's death and of life for him and John after that tragic event. It seemed that much of this information was being shared for the first time. Alan had been so afraid of upsetting John and himself. He was also worried that Maggie would not understand and might get cross and impatient if he harked back to the past. As Alan and John reminisced, the family listened and were moved by what they heard. John spoke very little but put his father right on certain facts and dates.

It was obvious that John had a lot of feelings and memories locked up inside and that it was difficult for him to express these in the family meeting, so my child psychotherapist colleague, Nick, offered to see John on his own to give him an opportunity to explore these hidden feelings in a less exposing situation. Rather to our surprise John agreed to come for this session the following week.

When Alan brought John for that appointment he handed Nick an envelope saying that the contents might be helpful. Inside was a sheaf of drawings and letters in childish handwriting. They were letters which John had written to Alan at the time of his mother's death. In them he wrote of his love for them both and his desperate wish that Alan should not mention Jill's name. He wrote, 'Do not say mum or Jill', and under a simple drawing of a woman he had drawn a headstone and written on it, 'I will always love my lovable mum'. In one note he wrote, 'It was a shame to hear', a direct reference to the way John had been told of his mother's death. Looking at these drawings and notes reminded John of that sad time. He agreed with Nick's comment that it was very hard to begin to get close to his new 'mum' when he had promised his real 'mum' to love her forever. Nick asked John if he had any of his mother's possessions and John said not but then remarked that his mum had always worn nice dresses. Nick was then able to say that maybe when John had taken the girl's underwear he was looking for comfort, for a sense of being back close to his mother. Perhaps he would have liked to keep some of Jill's things to have comforted himself with them. John nodded agreement.

The letters held another clue as to why John had remained so locked into himself. He had written to Alan, 'Do not be angry – I love you very much – do not shout or be cross', and other similar messages. All children go through phases of more or less affection for one or other parent. It seemed likely that at the time of his mother's death John was deeply attached to her and had fantasies of excluding his father from their relationship. After her death John was dependent on his father for his emotional security and so dared not allow these angry and rejecting feelings to surface lest his father retaliate. The relationship had to be made safe at all costs and so John wrote these placating and reassuring letters.

John's repeated request to Alan not to mention Jill's name had been obeyed and so they had both silently agreed not to speak about her or their shared pain.

John had not been able to mourn his mother's death and could not therefore begin to make a relationship with Maggie. When Alan sent the letters with John to the clinic, he was giving John permission to speak about all these things and we were sure that this was essential if John was to recover.

Some weeks past before we next saw Alan and Maggie. We could hardly recognise them. Whereas before they had looked care-worn and unhappy, they now seemed young and relaxed. They told us the news. First of all, they had moved into a new house with enough space for each member of the family to be separate when they wanted. Secondly, John had begun to relate to Maggie and to join in family life. To Maggie's amazement he had called her 'mum' for the first time and the evening before this session he had given her a really affectionate hug. Maggie described the relief she felt that the vicious circle of John's rejection and her anger had at last been broken. She could now begin to respond with real warmth. Alan was no longer afraid that Maggie would leave him. In fact, now that he felt safer about sharing his feelings he could see there had never been a real danger of Maggie going. She told him quite straight that she loved him far too much to let John's problem spoil a 'good thing'. We asked if there were any things of Jill's in the new house and we heard that Maggie had safely kept a small trunk with some of Jill's personal items, including her wedding dress. Alan had a box in which were all the letters sent at the time of Jill's death, as well as documents from her life. Until this moment neither had wanted to refer to these things, afraid of upsetting the other. It was a relief to both of them to talk about this and see how much easier it would be for John when they could stop behaving as if they were treading on egg shells.

In the months that followed Alan made a special effort to find times to talk to John about their past life with Jill. John was delighted to see the letters and objects that reminded him of his mother and now he had them he no longer needed to seek solace from stolen garments. John needed his father to go over the details of Jill's death a number of times. They cried together and Alan acknowledged the truth of John's written statement, 'It was a shame to hear'.

John will probably always be a quiet, introverted person, very different from his half-sisters – but in his quiet way he now takes a part in family life. Maggie feels relieved to have permission from Alan to be spontaneous with John and he responds to her warm and direct approach – and no longer feels that in doing this he is betraying his own mother.

CHAPTER 10

'Should we force her to go to school?'

Some ways of thinking about separation anxiety

We shall now explore the reasons why some children find it so distressing to be parted from familiar adults, particularly over going to playgroup, nursery school and big school; and how the problem can erupt unexpectedly after some years, especially around the major move from junior to secondary school.

In Chapter 3, on sleep disturbance, I tried to show how some parents and babies find it difficult to tolerate the smallest separation without becoming distraught and terrified. To ease the situation they needed to build up good, positive experiences of being apart for short periods and coming back together again to gain confidence that they were all right. When it comes to going off into the big world of playgroup and school, similar problems can arise, particularly if the child's earlier experience of separating from parents has been a sudden or prolonged one.

Many children cope with the transition from home to playgroup or nursery by taking into the strange environment a favourite toy or familiar object which can stand in for the loved parent and induce a sense of security. Other children choose to leave their best loved toy in their parents' safe keeping, as if, magically, they are leaving a bit of themselves at home while the rest of them goes off to nursery.

It is not only the child who may be anxious about separating. Many parents admit to quite upsetting feelings when they first leave a child at playgroup or school. So it is not surprising that a child's ability to separate is often influenced by parents' reluctance to let go.

I was visiting a playgroup one bright sunny morning on the first day of a new term. Three new children were due to start and they had all visited the previous term so the room, the helpers and the toys were familiar. Sally and her mother arrived and were warmly greeted by the playgroup leader. I could see Sally's eyes going towards the sand tray and she gently pulled her mother in that direction. It seemed clear that Sally was intending to stay and play. Her mother had a brief word with the leader and then went over to Sally to say goodbye. What she actually said as she knelt beside Sally, with an arm tightly round her, was, 'Mummy is going now Sally, when mummy goes Sally must not cry or run after mummy, be a good girl and mummy will be back later, don't cry will you?' Roughly translated I think this really meant, 'I cannot bear to leave you here, my adored youngest child, I need to know that this upsets you as much as it upsets me, please give me a sign by crying, then I will feel better.' Needless to say Sally got the message hidden in her mother's words and after a few seconds hesitation rushed after her crying. At that point they both needed the skilled intervention of the leader to make it possible to be apart, she acknowledged that it was difficult and upsetting for the mother but reassured them both that they would be coming back together again in two hours. Then Sally and her mother could begin to build up good experiences of being apart and the joy of reunion.

A long way from home

Ben was quite a different kettle of fish, he was the third of four children and already going to a nursery in his home town in

Australia. His father was having a year of post-graduate study in England. After organising schools for the two older children, Ben's parents were really pleased to find a playgroup for him, as he had seemed bored at home and was often asking about his school in 'Straly'. There was a fourth child in this family, Molly, who was just 1. Ben was a physically large boy, who though only 3½ was more like a 5 year old. He had very little distinct speech but seemed determined and initially friendly. The family had been in this country for about two months and were all missing the sunshine and open air life they were used to. Ben's father was excited to be studying in London but his mother was feeling quite overwhelmed by the wet and windy weather, and she was really missing her circle of friends back home. Closed in with four quite young children in a rented house brought its own problems, and the thought of Ben being happily placed in a playgroup each morning took a weight off her mind.

Ben showed no distress when she left him and he immediately joined in co-operatively with the group of children playing with cars on the floor. He seemed able to share and take turns. At snack time he sat and ate his biscuits and had a drink and then at one of those moments when all the children were milling around while the tables were being moved and the toys rearranged, there was a piercing scream. As far as anyone could tell, Ben had pushed over a little girl who was quite shocked and very distressed. An adult helper kept an eye on Ben for the rest of the morning. The next day a similar pattern emerged. Ben arrived looking excited and dashed towards the toys. After a few minutes he and another little boy were arguing over who was going to have a particular car and Ben hit him extremely hard and was moving in to hit him again when the leader got hold of Ben and tried to take him to one side. At this Ben went berserk. The leader later said she felt he was like a wild animal and was quite frightened of what he might do to her. In the end he calmed down, but the adults all agreed that he needed watching the whole time. They were determined not to be beaten by Ben and saw him as a real challenge to their skills.

Ben's parents were, of course, upset to hear what had happened and were reassured by the leader's conviction that once he had settled down and felt safe in the group all would be well. Two mornings later after about an hour of energetic playing Ben had his drink and biscuit and then leant over to the child next to him and simply helped himself to her biscuit. She tried to retrieve it, whereupon Ben put his head down and bit her arm really badly. Her screams brought all the adults rushing over and Ben, quite enraged by now, needed two people to hold him and try to calm him down. The leader said she was sure Ben would have bitten her given half a chance. By now she had had several complaints from parents about Ben and she was feeling somewhat of a failure because it had reached the point where she was having to think of excluding Ben from the group. She had the whole group to care for and Ben's unprovoked attacks were too dangerous to the other children to be tolerated. I felt that Ben was making it clear that he could not cope with being in this group and it would be better for him to be withdrawn at this stage. I invited the whole family to come to the clinic.

The Dysons were a strikingly beautiful family. Paul, 8, and Kate, 6, were articulate charming children who drew and cut out enthusiastically, joining in the conversation in quite an adult way. Molly just sat on the floor grinning at whoever gave her attention. Ben was all over the place, he could not settle to any activity for more than a minute before he became desperate to take whatever someone else was playing with. At one point Mr Dyson had to intervene between Ben and Paul and Ben looked explosive. His father tried to talk him down and apply sweet reason but Ben was not listening. He looked so frustrated and enraged and there was no way of discharging the emotion. His speech was so slow and inarticulate that he could not say anything, all he could do was cry with rage. He moved towards Molly and in a flash Mrs Dyson scooped Molly off the floor sensing that Ben would vent his rage on her. Ben finally allowed himself to be put on his father's lap until he calmed down. I sensed Ben's plight. It seemed that he had no special place in the family. The parents had each other, Paul and Kate were friendly together, Molly was loved by them all but obviously mother's special person because she was the baby and still needed a lot of individual care and attention. On top of all this, it was clear that Ben was doubly disadvantaged, for not only was he a mere 3½, but he had such poor speech he had no means of letting anyone know how he was feeling. He felt so overwhelmed and helpless that he reverted to quite babyish ways of reacting. Paul and Kate made it clear that Ben was the bane of their lives, interfering and spoiling their things and that when he was really angry they were afraid of him. I felt Ben was lost in the family and had taken that lost feeling into the playgroup. He was also lost in terms of geography, for he knew he had another home in Australia and another school but he could not comprehend where they were and why he was not there. Mrs Dyson said that as far as she could tell Ben had been the most confused and upset by the move. He was feeling left out, muddled and upset and he could tolerate no frustration. His biting and rages were a very primitive infantile reaction to a stressful situation, and I felt he was giving clear indications that he should not be expected to cope in the playgroup. Mrs Dyson spoke of her own homesickness and her envy of her husband who was thoroughly enjoying his course in London. She felt she could not cope with having Ben at home all day, every day. It would mean watching that he did not hurt Molly and she thought he would be very bored.

We worked out a plan with a three-pronged approach. First of all Ben should be withdrawn from playgroup. Then the Dysons were going to find a registered childminder who had no other children to care for at that time. They would arrange for her to have Ben on two mornings a week and Molly for two mornings during term times. Because of Ben's poor speech I suggested he have a hearing test. Last, but by no means least, to help Mrs Dyson with her depression the couple agreed to arrange an evening out for themselves in the not too distant future, something they had not had since they arrived in this country.

It was a month before my next meeting with Mr and Mrs Dyson and I was immediately struck by the dramatic change in Mrs Dyson's appearance. She no longer looked so thin and exhausted, she was dressed colourfully and her eyes had come alive. The plan had been a great success. Ben really liked the childminder and had been thrilled to find out she had two dogs. On the day that Molly went to her Ben and Mrs Dyson had really enjoyable times together, including going on short train journeys just for the fun of it. Mrs Dyson said that she felt she and Ben were getting to know each other properly for the first time. Mr and Mrs Dyson had been to a concert and a meal out which they both enjoyed, but the most striking news was that Ben had started to talk. The Dysons felt that this had happened quite suddenly and given Ben the ability to say what he was feeling and thinking, so he no longer had to explode with frustration. They were staggered to hear Ben talk of his memories of home and his longing to go back.

Just before Christmas the playgroup leader had called in to give Ben the toys and sweets he would have had from Santa Claus. He was delighted but never asked if he would be going back, it was as if he knew what was best for him. He understood that he would go back to his own school in Australia and his parents had made a big paper spider with a leg for each day that the family still had left in England. Ben pulled off one leg each night.

Children starting full-time school at 5 will show a wide variety of responses to separation. Those children who have a good enough experience of consistent loving care, with manageable separations during the early years, will have developed a secure sense that they and their loved ones can manage to be apart from each other and feel all right.

Some children will have already experienced traumatic separations before they were able to cope emotionally and this can produce two rather different types of child. The first group develop an amazing ability to cope and be independent. They seem very capable and self-assured and fool themselves and the world that they do not need anyone. The second group react quite differently. These are the clinging, crying children who are obviously unhappy and cannot play or learn properly. Through their behaviour this group of children manages to draw attention to their plight. Of course, many children have brief periods when they become reluctant to go to school. Sometimes this happens when the going gets rough in school, upsets with friends, bullying, teachers being cross, problems with work. Different things can upset different children. It is important to listen to what a child says has happened and not dismiss it. It may be necessary to contact school, talk to the teacher or to the head. Most problems can be ironed out with a minimum of upset all round, so long as the adults are communicating and the child is being listened to. But sometimes a child becomes so anxious about going to school that everyone is at a loss to know what to do. It is a terrible ordeal for parents to take a child into school when he or she is screaming hysterically and clinging on to them. Even quite young children can become ill with fear, shaking, pale, tearful, and prone to severe abdominal pains. Older children may feel faint on the way to school and have to go home. Parents of such a child will be unsure what to do and have often tried everything before seeking help.

Why Jason had to stay at home

Jason was 6 when he began telling his mother that he did not want to go to school. To start with she took a sensible matter-of-fact approach, jollying him along and stressing what a good time he would have in school. She checked with his teacher who said that Jason was fine once he was in school and that he enjoyed all the activities and had a group of friends. He was never on his own in the playground. His teacher thought Jason one of the happiest and most able children in his class. Everyone was deeply puzzled by his outburst of crying each morning. Sometimes he had to be prised out of his mother's arms and his screams rang out across the playground while she went miserably towards home. Jason had an older brother, Peter, who was in junior school in the adjacent building. He was a much shyer and more anxious child than Jason but he had never had a worry about going to school.

I arranged to meet Mr and Mrs White with both the boys to try and work out with them what these panics were really all about. I put five comfortable chairs in a circle and in the middle a table with coloured pencils and lots of paper and a box full of toy animals. As soon as the family came in I saw Jason look longingly at the toys and yet he stayed close to his mother, standing by her chair leaning against her whispering into her ear. Peter sat in the big chair and seemed rather grown up for 9. Mr White wore dark tinted glasses which gave the impression that he was hiding and he looked very care-worn and pale. He was obviously a lot younger than his wife and she took the lead in the session telling me about the problem with Jason refusing to go to school and how worried she was becoming. It sounded as though Mrs White was taking total responsibility for coping with the problem, so I asked Mr White if he sometimes took the boys to school. He murmured something about never being there because he worked in London, and then Mrs White said that Jason would not let his father do anything for him. The story unfolded. Mr White was in his words 'a crisis drinker'. He would drink little for months and then in the face of some stress at work or home he would go on a binge which always resulted in a protracted verbal row with his wife, during the course of which she would threaten to leave. After these episodes he was full of remorse, she stayed, and life would go rather better for several months. The last binge had been over the recent new year just before Jason's problems started. On this occasion Mrs White had decided that she was no longer prepared to put up with the abuse from her husband and had left the house overnight, returning in time to get the boys up in the morning. I said I thought it must have been very frightening for the boys and both nodded their agreement. Mr White began to cry, saying how deeply sorry he felt and how he wished he and his wife could get back to the happy times they had before the boys were born. Jason's panic about going to school was easily understood as a terror that something would happen to his mother while he was away. Either she would be attacked by Mr White or she would disappear. While we talked Jason began to play with the animals, making a fence around the wild animals (keeping people and feelings safe) and putting the animals in pairs as if lining up for Noah's Ark, perhaps showing how much he wanted his parents to be a couple. I felt it was important for both the boys' peace of mind to hear their parents owning the problems in their marriage. Mrs White was able to say clearly to Jason that she did not need him to stay at home, that she and dad were going to try and sort out their problems. Mr and Mrs White agreed to a number of sessions to look at their difficulties and Jason was able to return to school feeling much safer.

It is interesting to see how one child in the family will show the disturbance while another is apparently symptom free. The upset child may be doing the family a great service by drawing attention to something which is going wrong. In the White family, Jason could be said to have got his parents the help they needed. Peter, I was told, 'was a very good boy', but in the family meeting he revealed how deeply frightened he was, and how he dealt with his fears by being extra good and not burdening his mother. It was as if Jason was carrying the upset for them both and as he was less afraid to show his feelings, he was presented as the disturbed child when the real problems lay in the marriage.

The 'Little Mother' who could not go to school

Janet should have been at secondary school for three terms at the point when I heard about her problem. In fact, she had hardly been at school at all. She had gone to school for about three weeks in the first term but her attendance had gradually got worse until in the summer term she had not been in school on a single day. The Education Welfare Officer had visited the family and was struck by the parents' obvious wish to get Janet to school, but their helplessness in the face of Janet's declared refusal to go. He referred them to the clinic.

Janet, 12 years old, arrived with her parents Mr and Mrs Long,

Lloyd 9 and Sharon 7. Janet looked terror struck. She was a thin girl, pale and tired and close to tears. Lloyd and Sharon were cheerful noisy children who ran to the play materials ignoring their parents' requests to sit still and be quiet. I started by asking the family if everyone knew why they had come to see me. Lloyd announced that it was because Janet was 'naughty' and would not go to school. Mr Long stated that he and his wife were at the end of their tethers and Janet was causing rows between them. By this time Janet was weeping silently. Mrs Long looked rather accusingly at me and said they had only just managed to get her to the clinic – 'she won't go anywhere now, it's a job to get her out of bed'. I guessed (correctly as it turned out) that Janet might be very frightened about what we were going to do about the problem. She whispered that her parents had said she might have to go to boarding school if she did not go back to her school. I told her that I was not someone who sent people anywhere and that I was there to help them all to understand how the problem had come about, and why Janet had been so frightened about leaving home. Janet's parents told me what a clever child she had always been. She had enjoyed junior school and had friends, many of whom had moved on to her secondary school with her. Mr and Mrs Long had been up to the school on many occasions hoping to uncover the reasons for Janet's unhappiness, but the school was as baffled as they were. She had no problems with the work or with friends and no one at school could understand it at all. Having made sure that there were no serious difficulties at school, I decided to focus on Janet's experience of being separated from her parents. The step from familiar junior school to unfamiliar secondary school seemed to have been too much for her. I felt sure that something must have been too much for Janet when she was little. We talked about the life of this family and gradually the colour came back into Janet's cheeks and she began to join in the conversation.

Mrs Long was pregnant with Janet before she and Mr Long decided to marry. When Janet was 2 Mrs Long was admitted to hospital in the night with a miscarriage. She was away for three days during which time Mr Long took Janet to his sister's house for the daytime and collected her each evening. She had seemed fine. When Mrs Long came home she felt that Janet had not even noticed that she had been away. Mrs Long recalled how upset she had been at not seeing Janet while she was in hospital and then when Janet seemed so calm on her return she was puzzled and a bit sad. Janet started in a playgroup when she was 3, she settled quickly which was a relief to the Longs who by this time were expecting another baby. Lloyd was born two weeks after Janet started playgroup and Mrs Long was only away for forty-eight hours. She recalled Janet's delight over the new baby and how grown up she seemed, helping to fetch and carry for her mother and showing no signs of jealousy.

Janet moved on to big school when she was nearly 5 and soon afterwards Sharon was born. For a few days Janet had cried when her mother took her to school but this had passed off and she soon insisted on walking to school by herself. Mr and Mrs Long both remembered how helpful and grown up Janet seemed. Mrs Long had been a bit depressed after both Lloyd's and Sharon's births and had wished that her own mother had been nearer so she could have been a support. As it was, Mrs Long was relieved that Janet enjoyed being so supportive.

I asked them all how they expressed their cross upset feelings. While Lloyd and Sharon laughed about their fights and tempers, Janet's eyes filled with tears. Mrs Long said she felt safe getting cross with 'those two' but felt awful being cross with Janet. When Mr Long got cross with Janet for not going to school Mrs Long felt she had to intervene to protect her from his criticism and anger. It seemed as if Janet and Mrs Long were unable to separate because of the unacknowledged resentment and anger that lay hidden between them. When Mr Long tried to assert himself, he and Mrs Long ended up arguing and that added to Janet's sense of danger and fear of things falling apart. Although Mrs Long seemed to think that Janet needed protection from Mr Long, I got no sense that he was actually doing anything at all cruel or inappropriate. There was something else that needed understanding before they would be together enough to get Janet back to school. Luckily it was half term by this time, so there was time to have one meeting with the parents to explore this further. Before the end of the first session both Mr and Mrs Long agreed that Janet would return to school on the first day after the half term. It was very important for Janet to hear that her parents were agreeing about this and that they were going to be in charge of her. I said we all knew it would be difficult for Janet but that the longer she was away from school the harder it would be to go back. All through her life Janet had been very independent and never bothered her parents but now she was showing how much she needed their care and understanding. They would look after her and make sure she got to school, they would also make sure that both her form teacher and the head teacher understood that Janet was coming back to school and that no special fuss should be made, but that if she felt upset she should be able to go and talk to someone and not be sent home. Janet said she liked her form teacher and would ask to see her if necessary.

When Mr and Mrs Long came to see me without the children, the missing piece of the puzzle fell into place. I asked them about their early relationship and Mrs Long, with difficulty, revealed her secret dread that Mr Long had only agreed to marry her because she was pregnant. She felt that she had tricked him into it because she had wanted him so much. They had never talked about this, now they began to do so and Mr Long was staggered to hear what his wife had thought all those years ago. He told her he had never felt tricked by her and that he had made up his own mind to get married. Mrs Long had been thinking about the past and could see that she had had her own emotional reasons for going along with Janet's so-called 'independence'. In a way she had leant on Janet for support and confidence for herself while protecting her daughter from what Mrs Long had thought were Mr Long's angry feelings towards her.

It was a moving session in which these two parents were able to reassure each other and get together over coping with Janet. They could also understand how deeply Janet had buried her need for love and attention which had erupted in the current crisis. Mrs Long was happy to let her husband help in what would undoubtedly be an upsetting business getting Janet back to school. But they had both decided she was going back on the Monday after half term. We discussed all the possible problems and strategies for coping. I stressed how important it was for Janet to know that whatever happened on Monday she was definitely going to school. Mr Long assured his wife that he would be there to share it all. I arranged to see the whole family again for an after school appointment on the third day of the second half of the term.

When the family arrived the following Wednesday, I heard that Janet had been very tense and tearful for the twenty-four hours before she was due back. On the Monday morning she had felt sick and had tummy ache and eaten nothing. Mrs Long felt so sorry for her but reassured by our discussion she now believed that it was important for Janet to get back to school, however awful she felt. Because Mrs Long allowed her husband to share the problem she felt less overwhelmed and he felt less criticised and undermined. Mr Long had said he would take Janet by car on the first morning and then she could arrange for a friend to call for her the next morning. Mrs Long said goodbye to a most unhappy Janet. When Mr Long got her to the school gates he offered to take her in but she chose to wait until she spotted two friends, they seemed really pleased to see her and Janet went in with them. Mr Long went straight to work and telephoned his wife with the news. They had broken the pattern, everyone was relieved.

Now that Janet was back in school we could begin to work on some of the issues that had contributed to her separation anxiety. Most importantly, the fact that Janet had hidden from her parents and herself her need to be cared for and protected. Also her jealousy of her brother and sister which had been buried beneath the false, coping capable 'little mother' personality. Janet had been independent too soon, her crisis over going to school had provided an opportunity for her needs to be seen and met so she could catch up on her own development and move more safely towards a real and healthy independence at the right time. Everyone in the family had to make changes and see things differently, but they were willing to do this and Janet responded by settling back at school and doing well. She always found it upsetting going back after holidays but now she felt safe that her parents would help her over this hurdle.

CHAPTER 11

Stealing

Parents who discover their child has been stealing are bound to be very alarmed and worried. They may see the road ahead as leading to delinquency and a prison career. All their doubts and uncertainties about how they have raised their children will surface and can cause a great deal of unhappiness and mutual recrimination.

What may be termed 'borrowing' or 'using' in one family can be seen as 'stealing' in another. Sometimes it is not the importance or value of the object itself which is the main cause of upset, but rather the way in which it was taken. Parents can often tolerate the sort of stealing which seems to occur on the spur of the moment, but find it very hard to bear the thought that the child has premeditated the act and waited for the right moment to occur.

I once had a desperate telephone call from a mother who said her son had started stealing and she was frantic with worry about 'where it would lead'. He was only 5 and the stealing consisted of taking chocolate drops from the sweets drawer without asking. At one level it seemed a great fuss about nothing, and yet I could not ignore her distress. We talked on the telephone for quite a long time and she revealed that her husband was serving a prison sentence for burglary. What she was really frightened about was that her son was going to follow in his father's footsteps and she wanted help to avoid this repetition.

How parents react to their child's stealing will depend on so many factors, not least on their own internal standards of right and wrong, which will have been learned in their own early childhood. Most people have some memory of taking something, however trivial, from someone else, when they were young. Most can recall the dangerous but exciting feeling of doing something naughty and wrong, and then the guilt and anxiety about being found out, sometimes the lies that are needed to cover up the truth which can turn a small incident into a large one, with all sorts of ramifications. They may recall the feelings of shame and guilt that they felt when loving adults became upset and disappointed in them. Parents, who when they were children may have struggled hard to be 'good', may be quick to try and jump on behaviour in their own children which reminds them of their own forbidden wishes.

Stealing from within the home can take many forms. At one extreme is a child who constantly raids the biscuit tin and larder, having repeatedly been told to ask first – the sort of child who goes into his brother's or sister's room and 'borrows' things which seem to end up lost or broken, who never makes allowances for other people's needs and wishes but has to have his own needs met immediately, even when this incurs everybody's anger. None of this behaviour is secretive but very much out in the open and leads to a high level of annoyance and irritation in everyone. Parents faced with this sort of child will need very firm family rules to help protect the various members' rights to privacy and security. Possessions and territory need to be clearly defined and ways should be found to help the child make restitution and repair the damage that he may have done.

Food and love

Most people see food as a very fundamental comforter. People in love seem to survive on fresh air, but harassed parents and worried children may seek solace in the kitchen. From the earliest days of life an infant experiences the mother's love through being fed and safely held. For a little while the mother may put her baby's needs before any other, but then, gradually, the wider demands of life impinge and the baby will need to develop the capacity to tolerate a certain amount of frustration while he waits to be fed and when new foods are introduced. When this goes well the child will have an optimistic feeling that his world and the people in it will meet his need to be loved. For other babies and children difficulties can develop which result in a pessimistic view of the world in which they feel that their needs may not be met and they will be unloved. Such children will long to return to the earlier stage of life when their urgent needs were immediately satisfied. If food represents love, then a child taking food to eat alone may well be feeling unloved and miserable.

John was 7 when his mother began to notice crumbs in his bed. She discovered that he would go to the kitchen in the night and take whatever he could find to eat, and on occasions bottles of milk too. He had always been a quiet, rather withdrawn boy, but not a worry and certainly never naughty. He had a sister of 4 and a brother of 4 months. His parents were tired and worried about money, and John's mother's reaction to John's stealing was to be very cross indeed. He withdrew even more and continued to steal food and drink. When the family came for help with this we were able to see the stealing in a different way – as John seeking comfort on his own rather than turning to his mother. John had felt pushed out when he was 2 and his sister was born, and rather than fight for his position as mother's first baby he had been 'good' and co-operative. When the third baby came along he gave up hope of getting close to her and sought comfort in his secret eating. Instead of being cross his parents now got together to work out how he could have more of his mother's loving care. She organised her time so that she could be available for him to have a cuddle, look at books and enjoy just being together. This practical approach made a dramatic change in John. He became more lively and demanding and now his parents could see this as 'good' rather than 'bad'. He no longer needed to take the food.

John's mother had been the eldest of five children in her family and she had felt pushed out too, but the feeling had been buried. She came to see how like John she had been – afraid to ask for comfort for herself. So not only John benefited from the time spent working out what was going on, but his mother, in meeting *his* emotional needs, also made up some of what *she* had lost. John's dad had been trying to 'make a man' of John – to interest him in football and fishing. Now he could understand that John was not ready for these hobbies, so he helped him by taking the younger two out while John had time with his mother. Family life became richer and more enjoyable for everyone. By catching up on what he had missed John used the loving care to come out of his crisis and grow up into a boy better able to enjoy what life had to offer.

Stealing money

Parents may be even more worried by the child who takes money, usually from them and often in a way which avoids discovery for some time. When accused he will deny and lie in such a convincing way that the parents may begin to doubt their own positions. If he finally admits it there may be tearful promises that it will never happen again. Then it does happen again and the parents are plunged into despair and may feel helpless and very angry. By the time families come for help over this sort of stealing there will probably have been several episodes. Parents will have tried everything – punishment, talking, making the child pay it back, etc. They will have been convinced by their child that each time it is the last, but it never has been. At this point it is helpful to see stealing as being to do with the expression of two powerful forces – love and hate. In stealing from parents (usually the mother) the child is stealing the love (as symbolised by the money) and attacking or punishing the loved and longed-for person at the same time. Parents are more likely to feel and respond to the attacking part of the action than to recognise the underlying longing to be loved. Their understandable anger and punitive response may go to confirm the child's view of himself as no good and unlovable. This sort of stealing is definitely a 'cry for help' and should not be ignored. It is such an upsetting attack on the parents that they may need a lot of support to summon up the emotional strength to resist the temptation to attack back.

Chris had repeatedly taken money from his mother's purse to buy sweets and crisps to indulge himself. His parents were caring and thoughtful people and he had a sister five years younger. His parents were open to Chris about their sense of being let down by him, disappointed and hurt. Each time they had discovered he had stolen from them there were tearful and heartfelt promises that it would never happen again.

In my first meeting with the whole family I was struck by the excitement Chris showed when talking about his sister's birthday party which was the next day. His eyes lit up when he told me of all the delicious cakes and sweets they would be having. At the next meeting a week later I heard that Chris had not been allowed into the party 'because he was too noisy' but had a friend his own age up in his room. Chris was in tears as we talked about his longing for all the little cakes and tiny sweets. He clearly felt that his little sister was getting all the 'goodies'.

His parents talked about his early childhood and how he started school just before his sister, Clare, was born. As Chris was a very intelligent boy they had thought the stimulation of school would appeal to him – but he had become more and more unhappy, friendless and unable to concentrate. Chris's stealing brought the family for help.

When I met the parents without the children they told me that Chris had been an unplanned baby and life had been very stressful in his early years. Chris's mother came from another country, felt isolated and homesick. Also they had both hoped for a daughter. By the time Clare was born everything had improved and the family were much happier – Chris's jealous, hungry feelings went underground and he became increasingly unhappy and difficult to manage. A vicious circle built up in which Chris felt unloved and behaved in such a demanding and provocative way that his parents were constantly getting irritated and cross, which played into his sense of being no good. This also affected his life at school, where he was quick to take offence and got into fights. Matters were not made any easier by the fact that Clare was a gorgeous little girl who enchanted everyone she met.

We met altogether several times and the parents talked openly with both children about those early years – acknowledging how difficult it had been for them all – including Chris. They began to feel more in touch with the good things in him and to praise him instead of constantly criticising. His mother helped him bake cakes and eat as many as he wanted! She felt less angered by his greediness and gradually they began to feel a little happier. At Clare's next party Chris was able to take part as a big brother who helped. He could be with the little ones and eat the food but at the same time he now enjoyed being parental, pretending to be grown up.

Gradually Chris learnt that when he feels hurt and hard done by he can come out with it – so there is more healthy rivalry between the children. I remember the day when I heard for the first time that Clare had been difficult – if she could be 'bad' as well as 'good' then Chris could be 'good' as well as 'bad' – a much happier state of affairs for everyone.

Stealing and insecurity

Children whose early lives have been disrupted are particularly prone to stealing from their parents, sometimes years after the events which caused them to feel insecure or rejected. Michelle was 12 when her foster parents realised she had been stealing quite large amounts of money over many months. Michelle had lived with them since she was 3, but before that had had a very insecure life, moving between various relatives and foster homes, until being permanently placed with Mr and Mrs Bishop, her foster-parents, with whom she had a close and loving relationship. The Bishops had a natural son of 16, and a daughter of 10 and they were always in demand by their local fostering officer to take short-term foster-children, many of whom were very upset and demanding. When they discovered that Michelle had been stealing they both sat down with her to talk about it, to try and understand with her why it had happened and to work out strategies to avoid repetition. Being experienced foster-parents, Mr and Mrs Bishop knew that stealing was a sign of insecurity. They found time to talk with Michelle about how she was feeling in her life generally, the fears and anxieties she had about her position in their family and her natural family, with whom she still had some contact. They reassured her of her place in their family and in their affections. They knew she was envious of their natural daughter, just for being their own, as well as for her various talents. They reminded Michelle of her own positive attributes and reassured her of their love for her. They talked with her about her past, answering her questions fully and going back to letters and photos from her early life, which she had often seen, and yet needed to see again and again. They discussed money as a practical issue too and had a family rethink about pocket money and the payments they gave for extra jobs.

It was not realistic to expect Michelle to pay back the whole amount that she had taken, it was impossible to be accurate about that anyway, but they suggested jobs she could do to repay symbolically the stolen money. The Bishops were careful to make these tasks ones she could do well so that it would not be punishment, but rather an opportunity to improve her self-esteem. The Bishops knew it was likely that Michelle would steal again, so they told her that when she next felt tempted to take money she should go to one of them quickly and tell them, then they could help her to stop. They also took the obvious precaution of not leaving a lot of money lying around. Mrs Bishop knew that Michelle was very money conscious. She liked handling money and counting it, so she gave Michelle the responsibility for keeping account of the cash in her own house-keeping purse. Each morning and evening Michelle could empty the purse, sorting out the various denominations of coins and notes, and entering them all in a cash book which Mrs Bishop bought especially for the purpose. The Bishop's whole approach had been to include Michelle in tackling the problem of her stealing, to see it as a shared problem which they all needed to overcome and which stemmed from her feelings of insecurity and not from any failure to know right from wrong. They helped her to find ways to make reparation and so be forgiven.

Protection rackets?

Alice, who was only 5, stole money from her parents to buy sweets to give to the bigger children in the school playground. She said they had threatened to beat her up if she didn't do this, and she was terrified. Fortunately her mother found out what was going on and contacted the head teacher, who dealt with the matter at once, both by talking firmly to the four protection racketeers (all 6 year olds!) and by telling Alice to come to her at once in the future if she was ever frightened or worried.

Nick's mother was contacted by another mother who thought it odd that her son was coming home with £5 notes, saying that Nick was 'handing them out in the playground'. Nick was an attractive bright boy of 9 with no apparent problems.

I met the family and learned that the offence had come to light during the first school term in which Nick had not had his older brother Sam with him, Sam having moved up to secondary school. I heard that Nick had always been in Sam's shadow. Sam had taken Nick to and from school and protected him in the playground. Consequently Nick had never really learned that he could stand on his own feet. On the first day of term he had swiftly handed out 10p pieces to a number of children – protection money where protection was neither needed or demanded, for no one was asking Nick for money. The amounts had increased until the day he had handed out £5.

In the family meetings we explored the origins of Nick's feeling that he could not cope in the playground and mingle easily with the other children. I learned that the whole family had overprotected him since he had nearly died from pneumonia and bronchitis at 6 months. His sense of not being able to cope stemmed from this anxious overprotective attitude. The episode with the money had brought to light Nick's dilemma about independence. To help him Sam was encouraged to let Nick stand on his own feet and gave him tips on dealing with 'bullies'. Nick's parents gave him increasing independence, allowing him to go to Cubs and to the town with friends as well as joining in a school journey. Nick began to see that the world was less dangerous than he had thought.

Stealing outside the home

Parents who can tackle the problem when it arises in the family may be much more upset when it gets outside into the school or the wider community. It is important to remember that teachers, particularly in primary schools, are very used to dealing with the children who, like squirrels, collect rubbers, pencils and other little objects from school to take home and hoard. Young children may have grasped the idea that it is wrong to take things belonging to other people, but boxes of brightly coloured pencils in the teacher's cupboard seem to belong to no one in particular. Children need to learn that these belong to all the children and should be helped to return the 'borrowed' items, and that can be the end of the matter.

In older children the most common stealing is done as part of a small group in which the main motive is showing how intrepid and brave they are. Being caught once is often enough to put the youngster off. But sometimes a stealing offence is an indicator of deeper and more complex problems which cannot be solved just by punishment.

Alan was only 14 but 6 feet tall. His friends were all 16 and he longed to be accepted by them. One day they dared him to steal a box of tapes – he was caught and his parents were contacted by the store. They were puzzled, upset and ashamed and they worried about the influence he might have on his brothers of 11 and 9. They asked for a family meeting. Even before this had taken place Alan had repeated the offence in another shop and again was caught and this time the police were involved. On both occasions the older boys had run off abandoning Alan.

When I met the family I soon heard that Alan was not the father's child. The parents had met and married when Alan was 2. It gradually became clear that Alan's desperate longing to be accepted by the older boys was really about his wish to be accepted by his stepfather.

The more trouble Alan got into the more angry his stepfather had become. He really loved Alan and was deeply hurt by what he saw as Alan's rejection of him through not obeying his rules. The picture was complicated by his mother's feelings of guilt that 'her' son was being a problem when 'their' sons were not. As we talked about this together Alan was able to share his feeling that his stepfather was not proud of him. The outcome of this was that his stepfather began to treat him more like an older son, valuing his opinion and asking for Alan's help with difficult jobs. Alan no longer needed to seek approval from the older boys. He chose friends of the same age and was generally much happier.

Stealing as a defiant gesture

Deborah was suffering the burden of being held in high regard by parents and teachers. She was 17, good at everything and destined for academic success. One lunchtime she walked into a large chain store with two girls who had already been caught shoplifting and within minutes she was stopped by the store detective and her parents summoned. They were horrified and tried to blame the other girls' bad influence, but Deborah was determined to be responsible for her own actions. Then her parents took the line that she must be working too hard, and she should make an appointment to see their doctor to get a tranquilliser. Again Deborah stood her ground. In the end she came to the clinic with her parents and in two difficult and confronting sessions told them of her wish to be like other girls, to go out to discos, wear make-up and not spend all her time studying. She felt that the brazen act of shoplifting had been the only way to get them to see what a corner she felt she was in – as if only a great shock to the family system could lead to any change.

All the children described in this chapter had used stealing to show that they were upset. Each needed to be understood in his or her context, not just punished. Stealing really is a cry for help and if parents can hear the cry, the child can be rescued.

CHAPTER 12

Divorce

Some common problems for parents and children

As divorce becomes easier, quicker and cheaper to obtain, more and more marriages are breaking up. In 1984, 149,000 children were directly affected by their parents' divorce, and if present trends continue one child in every five born in 1987 will have to cope with parental divorce before the age of 16. Just because there is a lot of it about does not mean it is any easier for the children who are caught up in their parents' divorce. There are no hard or fast rules which can apply to every situation – so much will depend on factors which vary from family to family, and from child to child.

The effect on children of the breakdown in their parents' relationship will be influenced by the quality of family relationships before the split-up. Was it a sudden, unexpected separation? Or had there been months or years of increasing bitterness, perhaps with verbal or physical violence? Had the children been drawn into the battles between the parents, or at the other extreme been kept completely ignorant of the difficulties?

Children at different stages of emotional development will have widely differing reactions when their parents get divorced, and the way their parents need to talk to them about the situation will depend very much on the age and stage of emotional maturity that each child in the family has reached.

Although every child's experience will be unique to him or her, there are some aspects of the situation which are common to most children.

1   Children nearly always prefer to have their parents together and continue to hope for a reconciliation, even when parents have been apart for some time or are actually divorced.
2   Children often feel guilty, to a greater or lesser extent, about their parents' divorce.
3   Children often idealise the absent parent, while the parent who has care and control will pick up a lot of the angry, hurt feelings. This can be hard to bear on top of all the upset that will have been around with the partner.
4   The opposite can happen too: the absent parent becomes the bad one on whom all angry feelings can be placed. This splitting of the good and bad feelings is the child's way out of an intolerable emotional muddle. In the long run, he should be helped towards a more balanced view of the good and bad in both parents as well as in himself.
5   Children may remain sad or angry about the divorce and being separated from the absent parent, even though their parents are relieved, and perhaps much happier, as a result of separation and divorce.
6   The parent who is carrying a lot of guilt for the failed marriage may overcompensate for this by indulging the child in all sorts of ways, so that the divorce becomes the excuse for not tackling normal family problems in an effective way.
7   Children who are used as a channel of communication between warring parents will suffer.
8   It can often get forgotten, in the upheaval of divorce, that just because the partners are no longer in a relationship they both continue to be parents to their children.

Some children make no bones about being hurt, or angry, or relieved, or whatever it is they feel when their parents divorce. Others bury their feelings, sometimes for months or years, which makes it difficult for their parents to understand what is going on and to offer appropriate help.

'He's afraid I will leave him too'

Brett was only 3 when his father left on Christmas Eve to live with another woman. His mother, Mrs Sherratt, was not surprised because she had always felt the marriage had been rather 'half-hearted'. It was a very calm separation, and it seemed that Brett hardly realised his father had gone. He would visit him regularly at the grandparents' house and never mentioned him in between these visits. Some months later Brett's kitten was run over on the street outside his house and to Mrs Sherratt's surprise, he wept unconsolably and clung to her for several days. He became upset at bedtime, to the extent that she took him into her bed. He clung to her when she took him to playgroup and as she had not the heart to upset him anymore, she kept him at home. By the time they came to the clinic Brett was never apart from her, day or night, and had not been out with his father for several weeks. At our first meeting, Brett started to draw with fat wax crayons, big colourful swirls and patterns and shapes, which he said were his house and daddy's car. So we talked about daddy and Brett told me that his dad had 'gone to work' and that 'daddy can't live with us because there is no room'. Mrs Sherratt then explained how her husband had told Brett that this was the reason he was living elsewhere. She understood why her husband found it so hard to tell Brett the truth, for when he himself was a child his mother had placed him in a Dr Barnardo's home and kept his two sisters with her, the only explanation ever offered to him had been the excuse of no room at home. Mrs Sherratt agreed to help him to find a way to tell Brett the truth.

At about 3 years of age many children become intensely attached to the parent of the opposite sex. They long for an exclusive relationship with that parent and may feel that the same sex parent is a dangerous rival whom they would like to get rid of. At the same time the child loves the rival deeply and feels guilty about such angry, rejecting feelings. This can put the child in a real emotional conflict. Where the two parents are together, the child gradually has to come to terms with his or her position in relation to the longed-for parent, but where one parent goes away the situation can become very complicated. A young child believes his thoughts and wishes are magically powerful. He may feel that he has got rid of the rival and so suffer guilt and distress. In Brett's case the rival had left and Brett was confused and upset. He now had his mother's undivided attention day and night but when his father came to take him out Brett became upset and clung to his mother. It seems likely that at these times Brett feared that his father might punish him for, as it were, getting rid of him. Brett needed to be helped to see that no one in the family was as powerful and dangerous as he feared, for while he continued to see his father as a dangerous rival, he could not leave his mother or spend time with father. The whole picture was complicated by Mrs Sherratt's fear that if she encouraged him to visit Mr Sherratt or to stay at playgroup, he would become overwhelmed with terror that she too would leave him. What Brett really needed was the repeated good experience of being separated from her and finding that she was still there to come back to. The other important factor was Brett's genuine sadness at his father's leaving, and this had only erupted when the cat had died and Brett had been so inconsolable. Mrs Sherratt really did not want Brett in her bed but felt it would be cruel to insist that he went back into his own room, so she was relieved when I suggested ways of tackling this problem.

The following week two important events were planned and were to make Mrs Sherratt's task much easier. Firstly, she was taking delivery of a set of bunk beds, and secondly she and Brett were having a new kitten. Brett was excited about both events, but had spoken of his mother sleeping in the bottom bunk while he would be on the top. She had not felt able to disillusion him but as we talked she explained to Brett that when the beds arrived she would stay in her room and he would be on the top bunk, while the kitten could have a box on the floor in Brett's room. Mrs Sherratt agreed to stick to this plan. She knew that Brett would try every way to get her to sleep with him but now felt able to cope calmly with this. Brett had been drawing and playing while we talked over all these issues, he said little but listened to it all. The plan that Mrs Sherratt took away was fourfold: (1) she would talk to her husband about what to say to Brett, also she would help Brett to visit his father; (2) Brett would return to playgroup as before and Mrs Sherratt would check with the leader that he settled all right after she left him; (3) Mrs Sherratt would use the arrival of bunk beds to reorganise and redecorate Brett's room and talk to him about it being his room while her room would be only for her; (4) she would time his return to his own room with the arrival of the kitten. Life got back to normal and Brett's anxiety diminished markedly. He loved playgroup and saw his father regularly. Both parents now told him the same story about the separation and Mrs Sherratt had the emotional space she needed to develop her own interests and relationships.

'I feel like pig in the middle'

Where Brett's parents were on fairly good terms and could talk to each other, Colin's were definitely at war. Colin was 13 and his sister, Lucy, 9, when Lucy's head teacher referred the family because of Lucy's lack of concentration and poor performance at school. She was having extra help from a remedial teacher who said that, 'Lucy seems depressed and switched off and appears more like a 4 year old.'

The relationship between Mr and Mrs Allan had deteriorated over many years. Mr Allan had been quite fond of Colin but had showed no interest in Lucy from the day of her birth. Mr Allan was a very successful businessman who in a short time made a great deal of money, opening branches of his business throughout the country. In telling me about it, Mrs Allan could see that she had made herself a doormat and been used and abused by her husband. She had tolerated all sorts of humiliations. He would taunt her with her inadequacies and undermine what strengths she could muster.

By the time I first met the Allans the parents had been divorced for a year but apart for two. There had been terrible fights about money and at one time Mrs Allan had been unable to pay any bills and had been extremely worried. Mr Allan would ring Colin most Tuesday evenings but often forgot. He would then suddenly phone to say he was collecting Colin at a particular time and have him to stay. This incensed Mrs Allan on two counts. Firstly, she felt Lucy should go too and secondly she was furious that Mr Allan never asked if it was all right with her for him to take the children. As she was determined never again to be 'walked all over' by Mr Allan she refused to let Colin go away. The atmosphere in the home was awful. Colin and Lucy were totally unco-operative, fought constantly and were rude and offhand with their mother. When Colin was out Lucy would be affectionate towards her in a babyish sort of way. Mrs Allan felt the only way to have any peace in the home was to treat them like very young children. She did everything for them but then felt furious with them for apparently treating her just as her husband had done. Mrs Allan knew she was on a short fuse and that the person she was really most angry with was her ex-husband. She refused to allow Colin to see his father unless Mr Allan spoke to her first. Mr Allan told Colin, 'I am not prepared to speak to that cow.' It was an impasse.

At our first meeting it was clear that Colin and his mother were locked into a silent, angry impasse, while Lucy clung to her babyish ways to avoid being drawn in further to what was obviously a horrible situation. The first thing was to help them all to talk to each other – something they had not been able to do for months. The most surprising thing to emerge was Colin's understanding of his mother's position and feelings about the whole situation. She had no idea that he had such a grasp of the truth. She listened while he explained about his father's immaturity and unkindness to mother, how hurt he was at receiving so little real care and attention from his father, and his sense of injustice at his father's lack of love for Lucy.

He knew that his father used money to buy relationships. He explained so well the conflict that he felt between his wish to take all the material gifts his father offered and his reluctance to accept because of the pain this would give to his mother.

Mrs Allan had never felt that anyone had understood her point of view and was bowled over by Colin's grasp of the situation. She asked him why he had never talked to her before and he told her quite straight that she made it impossible because she was so angry all the time and nagged incessantly. He felt she gave him no opening. Mrs Allan admitted this and talked of her resentment at the demands the children made on her, her envy of her wealthy ex-husband who could please himself, and her rage with him for exploiting her in the past and ignoring her now. She admitted that she took out a lot of her frustration on Colin and Lucy. It was clear that both children would like the opportunity to spend some time with their father, but they were sympathetic to their mother's need to feel part of the planning of such a visit. She was not prepared to let them go unless the arrangement was made through her but Mr Allan was refusing to talk to her on the telephone, preferring to insult her to Colin. Colin's position between his parents was crucial and stressful. As he said, 'I feel like the pig in the middle, and it's not my fault.' Colin needed help. So we role-played a phone call between Mr Allan and Colin so that Colin could experiment with ways of coping with the two main difficulties. Firstly, his father's very unpleasant remarks about the mother, and secondly, his tendency to make arrangements with no reference to her plans for the family. Colin was relieved to have permission to be firm with his father and state quite simply that he did not like to hear those things about his mother, and that he was not prepared to continue the conversation unless they stopped. Over the second matter, Colin decided that the best way to manage both parents was to respond positively to his father's request to have him to stay by saying that they would both like to go (having checked with Lucy, of course), but he would just go and make sure that it was OK with mum. If his father said he need not bother to ask, then he would ignore him and ask mum anyway. Mrs Allan accepted this plan and all agreed to talk about it more at home and try not to get locked into battle stations.

Mr Allan did not phone for several weeks but when he did, Colin carried out the plan as practised and he and Lucy went away for a week. During this time Mrs Allan managed to enjoy herself for the first time for months. When the children returned with bags of goodies and new clothes she stopped herself exploding with anger and accusing their father of trying to buy their love, but was able to see that some of the things would be really useful. Rather to her own surprise, she found herself commenting positively on Mr Allan's current girlfriend, for laundering the children's clothes so well. She laughingly admitted that some months earlier if this had happened she would have assumed that they were criticising her standards of laundry and would have felt very put down and humiliated. As Mrs Allan felt calmer, she nagged less and the children began to be more caring and co-operative. Mrs Allan realised that she had turned to Lucy for the love and attention that she needed herself and that this had partly contributed to Lucy's reluctance to grow up. Mrs Allan needed to develop her own life outside the home and children and build up her confidence which had been shaky since childhood. Coming to the clinic had been her only trip into town for several months. She had felt quite panicky at the thought of doing things on her own but was determined to make real steps forward. She began to combine visits to the clinic with browsing in the shops and having a coffee out. She then took what was a very brave step and enrolled in a day-time class where she could improve her social skills, to give her self-esteem a much needed boost. At the end of the next term, Lucy's remedial teacher reported that Lucy was now really enjoying her schoolwork. She said, 'I can't put my finger on what it is, but she just seems more grown up.'

Divorce may only be part of the problem

Sally-Ann's mother had left the country without warning when Sally-Ann was 10 and Jeremy 8. She took Caroline, 2, with her. Mr

Casey had a very pressurised job and worked long hours. Reeling from the shock of his wife's sudden departure, he arranged for an elderly woman who lived nearby to come and be in the house when the children came home from school and so the family tried to get on with their lives. The children went to stay with their mother for one week of each school holiday. By now she was living with another man and looking after his two boys. Jeremy enjoyed these visits, but Sally-Ann developed quite severe asthmatic attacks and on one occasion she was admitted to the local hospital.

Sally-Ann became increasingly difficult. She was so rude and unco-operative that the childminder left and Mr Casey ended up employing a number of different people for different days. Sally-Ann cried at the slightest thing. She complained that nothing was fair and that her father did not love her but preferred Jeremy. Mr Casey became exasperated with Sally-Ann and although he wanted to understand and help her to feel better, he easily became irritated and angry at her provocative behaviour.

Sally-Ann wrote letters to her mother saying she loved her very much and wanted to live with her, but her mother often failed to reply and never took up the suggestion. Sally-Ann day-dreamed and wrote stories which were always a reflection of her own situation. In the stories the little girl and her mother were reunited and lived happily ever after. Her drawings too were all along the same theme.

In our first family meeting I asked what it was like when Sally-Ann and Jeremy stayed with their mother. Jeremy said it was fun, he liked sharing a bedroom with the other boys and he enjoyed playing with his little sister. Sally-Ann said that it was too noisy and that Caroline was 'a crybaby'. I commented that it must have been difficult to get time to be alone with mum. Sally-Ann looked tearful and nodded agreement. Then Mr Casey said something which put the whole problem in perspective, like shining a beam of light in a dark area, so that we could begin to understand. What he said was that the relationship between Sally-Ann and her mother had never been good since the day that Jeremy was born. Mr Casey was careful in what he said, not wishing to blame his ex-wife, but he spoke of her rejection of Sally-Ann whom she often hit, or put outside in the garden. He used to try to compensate for this rejection, which only made matters worse because Sally-Ann's mother became jealous of the attention that he was giving the child.

As the story unfolded in the session, the effect on them all was powerful. It seemed that although Sally-Ann had some memories of her mother's unkind and rejecting behaviour, it was too painful to acknowledge or face up to. She had chosen to idealise her mother, turning her into a fairy-tale princess. When she actually visited her and the relationship was not as she dreamed, she became upset and developed the physical symptom of asthma. All her rage with her mother had been re-routed on to the childminders and when she accused her father of not loving her, she was really trying to challenge her mother. As we sat and talked about these complicated matters, Sally-Ann told her father how bad she felt about herself, as if it were her fault that her mother had not loved her. Mr Casey regretted he had not taken action much earlier to help his wife, who on reflection he thought had probably been quite depressed after Jeremy's birth.

Over the weeks of our meetings he talked to the children about their lives before the divorce. He and Sally-Ann cried about it and shared the guilty and angry feelings that they both had. Jeremy seemed to have suffered less, probably because he felt more secure in his mother's affection. On the practical level, there was the question of whether or not Sally-Ann should visit her mother. Sally-Ann came up with her own solution. She said she wanted to go but not always with Jeremy. She would like to stay with her mother when the two step-children were away with their own natural mother. Mr Casey wrote to Sally-Ann's mother suggesting this and to everybody's surprise she agreed. It would be untrue to say that Sally-Ann enjoyed the visit, but she was able to salvage something from the limited relationship she had with her mother. She began to understand that it was not all her fault that things had not been happier between them.

Had Sally-Ann decided not to see her mother again a number of things could have happened. Having previously been idealised, her mother might well have become a very bad person in Sally-Ann's mind, someone to blame for everything that went wrong in her life, rather than taking responsibility herself. This could have coloured relationships later on, in which she might have experienced people as very black or white. By never seeing her again, Sally-Ann would have deprived herself of the chance to have something real, however small, of her mother. Through the sharing and reflecting that had started in the sessions and which Mr Casey continued at home, each of them could see the situation more clearly and acknowledge the difficult and different feelings that each of them had.

The dilemma of an 18 year old

Liz had told her friends she had a bottle of pills and felt like dying. It was the month before A-levels and a number of young people in her year were under a good deal of stress, but Liz was a high flyer. Everyone knew that she would do well. She already had a number of offers for places at university. She was popular, a natural athlete and the object of a lot of admiration. Her friends were baffled by her mood but caring enough to tell her year tutor, who referred her directly to the clinic.

It is easy to jump to conclusions and that is what I nearly did. Before she arrived I imagined, on the basis of the limited information that I had been given, that Liz was feeling like so many young people approaching A-levels, worried about the future and making the right choice of course and career. Her success might have become a burden that she wanted to be rid of but felt trapped by everyone's expectations of her. Perhaps she was upset by a relationship going wrong.

When she arrived and began to talk she made only a passing reference to the exams and school life. What was upsetting her so much was the atmosphere at home. About a year before this her mother had started her own business, a daring and exciting venture which needed more than full-time commitment. Liz's father also worked full-time and had to commute. Her older brother was in the army abroad. Liz complained that her parents were never around at the same time. Her mother had discussed her business venture very fully with the family before she went ahead and they had given their support, so Liz was feeling very guilty that now she wanted her mother to be more available. She longed for there to be times when she could relax and chat with both her parents – something she remembered doing in earlier years. I asked Liz if she had told her parents how she felt. She replied that she had tried to but sensed that she was not really getting through. Both her parents were affectionate towards her and reassured her of their love for her, both agreed they were preoccupied with work, but thought that Liz was happy with their flexible life-style. Neither of them was aware that Liz often cried for long periods in her bedroom. What Liz had not been able to do was talk to them together about how she felt. I wondered if a meal-time might provide the right moment, but she said it was months since they had eaten together. We worked out a strategy. Liz was to ask her parents to make a date when they could all sit down for a meal together. She would shop and cook for it but wanted them both there. When the evening came Liz was able to talk to them. She held nothing back and found herself crying a lot. She said how much she had missed the togetherness of earlier times. Only then were they able to tell her that for the past year they had been planning to separate, but had planned to keep this from her until after the exams were over. They had both organised their lives so that their paths crossed as little as possible. Now the truth was out Liz could begin to make sense of the many small changes she had felt in the atmosphere at home. Her parents had been so busy avoiding each other that she had got lost in the spaces between them. Liz was sad and sorry that her parents' marriage was ending but she could see that both of them were making plans which included her interests. They no longer had to pretend and the relief led to everyone feeling more relaxed and comfortable together. They all agreed to meet for a proper meal twice a week to talk about their plans and to support

Liz through her exams and be available together to hear what was happening in her life.

I only saw Liz again briefly. She popped in to tell me what had happened and said she felt OK now she knew what was happening, sad of course but she had her life ahead and she was looking forward to it.

CHAPTER 13

New families – new problems

After the inevitable upset and pain of divorce, some families settle down to a pattern of life with one parent and visits from, or to, the other, but many parents move quite rapidly into new relationships which lead to cohabitation or remarriage and the children go too. These 'new' or 'reconstituted' families can be very complicated set-ups to live within. Parents who come together with high hopes for a happy future for them and their children may be shattered to discover how difficult the change can be for some family members. There can be a sort of 'honeymoon' feeling in everyone and an excited hope that the bigger family will be fun and everyone will benefit. It may take some time before the problems emerge.

Mr and Mrs Johnson came to a family meeting because of their worries about Graham. A geneogram (Fig. 13.1), or family tree, helps to illustrate their new 'family'. Len and Mary both felt that everyone had settled down very well except for Graham. He was rude, and disobedient, particularly to Mary. He stayed out late and refused to eat in the same room as everyone else and had recently been involved with a group of friends in shoplifting. He was very angry about coming to the family meeting. He sat down muttering that he 'wasn't a nutter, no one was going to put him in a home, etc.'. Len explained that after his divorce both his boys had lived with their mother but she was under increasing stress and after a difficult year she decided to move back to live near her own family in Manchester. The boys went to live permanently with Len and although occasional letters passed between the boys and their

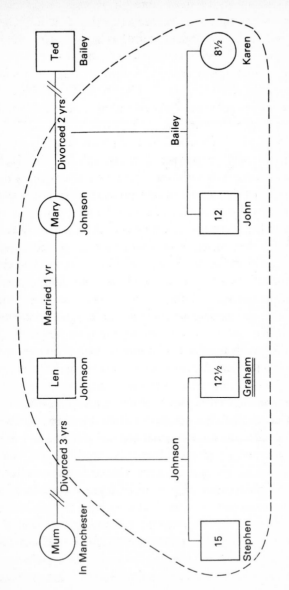

Figure 13.1 The Johnson/Bayley Family

mother, there was no expectation or wish to live with her. When Len and Mary married they all moved into Mary's house, which was on the other side of the town. Stephen had stayed at his original secondary school, while Graham started at his secondary school in the new district. He and John were in the same year and Len and Mary hoped that this would help them to forge a brotherly relationship.

As the family talked about their year together, it became clear that Graham was deeply jealous of his father's relationship with Mary, and of Mary's very close relationship with her son John, such a contrast to Graham's experience of being with his own mother. Mary had tried to get on with Graham but he was so rejecting of all her attempts that she decided to back off and let Len be the one to communicate with Graham. She felt that the only way to keep her sanity was to have as little as possible to do with Graham. Both Len and Mary felt their marriage, on which they had pinned so many hopes, was under threat. Mary had insisted that Len 'do something about Graham' as she was at the end of her tether. One idea in her mind was that Graham's mother should care for him, or if not that he should go to a boarding school. When I heard this I understood Graham's opening remarks about not wanting to be 'put in a home'.

In the first family meeting I asked each of them to state the worst and the best thing about being in their new family. Graham's response to this was immediate. The worst thing was having John trailing around everywhere and 'getting in my way'. The best thing was Mary's cooking. When he said this Mary's eyes filled with tears. This was the first nice thing Graham had said about her in a whole year and it meant a great deal. We looked in detail at Graham's remark about John 'always being in the way' and what emerged was that Graham was envious of John in all sorts of ways. In school, where they were in the same year, John was getting 'A's in everything and played in the band and was in the under-13 hockey team, while Graham was much less able and not interested in joining any club or society. He had always thought that he would follow Stephen into his school and he missed his friends from junior school. His other complaint was that John always had to be included in fishing trips with Len. For two years Graham and his father had spent a whole day each week fishing, something they both enjoyed and which gave them a special bond. Now Len had to do more in the home and with the larger family, so the fishing trips were fewer and Len always included John, much to Graham's annoyance.

As the family all shared more of how they saw the situation and the hopes and wishes they had for the future, they were able to identify the areas that could be changed and those that had to be accepted as unchangeable. Len and Mary made a clear statement to the whole family that they could understand that the children would sometimes feel fed up with the new family and long to put the clock back, but that they, Len and Mary, were committed to each other, and that nobody's impossible behaviour was going to drive them apart. Len and Mary both acknowledged that their hope of John and Graham being buddies was unrealistic and that both the boys would appreciate some space apart from each other. As Graham was unhappy at his school, Len decided to contact the head of Stephen's school and see if Graham could transfer. A lot of bargaining went on over the question of each child having time with their natural parent and Len agreed that he and Graham would have a monthly fishing expedition when John would not be included. Len encouraged Mary to behave spontaneously with Graham. If he made her cross then she would get cross and if he did something positive she would show her appreciation. This was much easier for Mary to do now that Graham had said something positive about her. There was a moving moment when Mary said that she had always felt that Graham had hated her and Graham looked up with tears in his eyes and said he had thought the same about her.

This family had begun to settle. There was a lot of work still to be done and inevitably there were ups and downs. With three adolescents in the family, all of whom had disrupted lives, there were bound to be some hiccups. The most important step in improving things was Len and Mary's acknowledgement there were some ways in which they would always be two families. Only when that was accepted could the new family begin to take shape in a real way.

Just how complicated can they get?

The straight answer to this question has to be, very complicated indeed. With the complexities can come confusion, particularly for younger children, who find it hard to comprehend the difficulties between various generations and the relationships between different family members. There are plenty of families made vast by remarriages and new unions, where everyone gets on with the changes, makes adjustments and feels enriched by the wide variety of relationships on offer. But some children get totally confused and unhappy when they cannot grasp who belongs to whom, and where they fit in. The Browns are a good example of this. It would be impossible to describe the family structure in words, so a geneogram, or family tree, will help (Fig. 13.2).

Chrissie's health visitor had called in to see the baby and in the general chat about the family Chrissie expressed her concern about Darren, whom she had looked after for the year that she and Alan had been living together. Darren would go to stay with his own mother (Cheryl) at weekends. This was a convenient arrangement because Chrissie's 11-year-old son was at a weekly boarding school and would have Darren's bed for weekends. Everyone agreed that Darren looked and behaved as if he were lost. Whether he was with his father and Chrissie or at Cheryl and Bob's, and even at school, he sat with his thumb in his mouth and a sad and perplexed expression on his face. He wet his bed every night and seemed listless and depressed.

The first meeting was with the family circled on the geneogram. Alan and Chrissie were explaining the various changes in their family structure and I became more and more muddled. I began to feel like Darren looked, so it was at this point that I suggested that we compile a family tree and the geneogram printed here is a tidied up

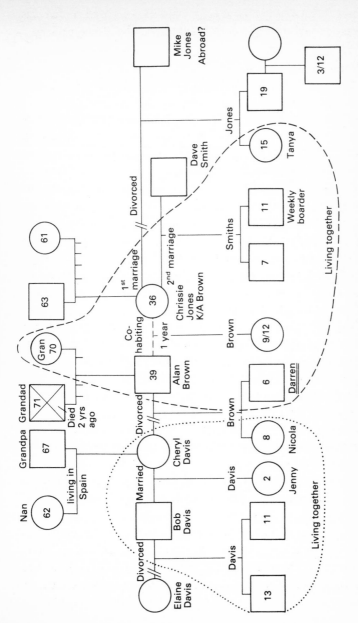

Figure 13.2 Darren Brown's Family Tree

version of the original, so that only the most essential information has been included. I asked Alan why Darren lived with him when Nicola had stayed with her mother. It was gran who told me in no uncertain terms that Cheryl had never looked after Darren properly and she and her late husband had cared for Darren and Nicola most of their early years when Cheryl was working. Gran said Cheryl had been a 'bad mother' to Darren and she was full of praise for all Chrissie had done to help him. It seemed that Darren's misery was partly due to his total confusion about how everyone fitted into the various parts of the family, coupled with the number of separations and losses which had been very traumatic and sad for him.

It took us three family meetings to complete the original family tree. Darren gradually began to show an interest and take part by asking questions and offering information. Lots of things emerged during these discussions, which seemed to have gone unnoticed in the general chaos of this family's life. The most important upset for Darren had been the death of his much loved grandfather when he was 4. Knowing how upset Darren would be about this, the adults had all agreed to tell him that grandad was ill and living in a hospital. Now he could be told the truth, which was a relief for them all. Not surprisingly, Darren had really known all along that his grandad was dead, but had never felt able to say so. Another major upset for Darren had been leaving his baby half-sister Jenny, whom he adored. Then after only a few months living with his father and Chrissie they had had a baby girl. It was hard for Darren to get close to this baby because Chrissie's older three were always there first and Tanya saw herself as a second mother and jealously guarded her relationship with the baby (I wondered if she was also quite jealous of her older brother's baby). Darren missed Nicola. They had been together all the time until Darren was 4 and Nicola had always been a caring big sister to Darren, who depended on her in all sorts of ways, particularly for the wonderful games which Nicola would create and in which he took part. When Alan and Cheryl had separated, there had been no arguments about Nicola staying with Cheryl, and Darren being with Alan. There were several reasons for this. Not only was gran's influence very strong but Cheryl had her hands full coping with Bob's two older children from his first marriage to Elaine. I had the feeling that gran's view of Cheryl was very negative and that Alan found it hard to confront her with a different opinion. I also felt that Darren was missing his mother, his sister Nicola and his half-sister Jenny and that Alan, Chrissie, Cheryl and Bob needed to sit down together and rethink the original plan. Fortunately they were on reasonably good terms and were prepared to meet all together to look at the options.

Darren's dilemma was clear – he wanted to be with Alan and Cheryl. Whatever was finally decided would be second best for him and that had to be clearly stated. If the decision was for Darren to go and live with Cheryl then Alan had to face his own sadness at not having his only son living with him. He would also need to deal with gran's upset and anger, and most important of all, help Darren not to feel guilty about choosing to live with Cheryl and not him. So Darren finally went back to live with Cheryl in that household, and after a few weeks I had a family meeting with Cheryl and Bob and the five children in their family. Darren had settled down quickly and lost his miserable perplexed look. He had learnt to use the telephone and could speak to his father, Chrissie and gran whenever he wanted and he went to stay overnight quite often at first. No one could put the clock back. Darren was always going to be sad that his parents were not together. He also misses gran's permanent presence but maybe without her he could build the relationship with Cheryl, his mother, whom gran had never liked. As to the bedwetting, it became less frequent as Darren settled down and cheered up. When I first met Darren I had thought he was full of unshed tears, which perhaps found expression through the wetting.

Darren had been the focus of concern on this occasion, but looking at the geneogram it would be possible to make some informed guesses about the worries or difficulties that each child in this complicated family might have to face. Compiling the geneogram had helped them sort out who came from which union, and how they were, or were not, related. This led to lots of questions being asked by the children, which the adults could be helped to answer. Darren certainly was not the only one to have been muddled and insecure.

CHAPTER 14

Adolescence

Parents' greatest challenge?

However successful and happy parents may have been throughout their children's babyhood and childhood, adolescence will probably throw up some real problems and challenges to the whole family. In some cultures there are initiation rites which make the line between childhood and adulthood much clearer. In our culture no such line exists and one of the dilemmas for parents of adolescents is just where and when to drawn the unseen line.

As well as coping with all the physical changes of puberty, the adolescent is struggling to find a true sense of self. He needs to find out who he is and how he fits into the world. He reassesses all the values and ideals of his parents which he has unquestioningly accepted throughout his childhood. The drive is towards becoming an individual separate from the parents, but at the same time there are also powerful longings to sink back into the dependent position of babyhood, to be cared for and not expected to cope with all the demands of life. These swings of mood and energy can leave parents baffled and exhausted for they never know from one day, or even one moment to another, whether the 15 year old they are dealing with is feeling like a 5 year old or a 25 year old.

Adolescence is a time of extremes in everything but it is not an illness, rather a phase of development, a journey from childhood to adulthood. Like many journeys it turns out quite differently from what was planned. The going is often tough and the adolescent may long to retreat to the comfort and security of the life he knew before the journey began. Parents cannot undertake this journey on behalf of their children, but they need to provide the base from which the journey begins and to which the adolescent can return for comfort, care and support.

While the adolescent is trying to find out who he is separate from his parents, he will need the support of his own age group to boost his sense of self, to give him the courage to challenge parental standards in all sorts of ways. It is much easier to be outrageous in a group than on one's own. How parents approach this phase of family life will depend on a number of factors, not least how they felt as adolescents themselves. If they were not able to negotiate this difficult period in their own growing up, then they will probably feel anxious coping with their own adolescent children. Some parents who, for whatever reason, never had a proper adolescence of their own may want to have it with their own children, to join them in their rebellion and cock a snook at parental standards that are reflected in society's rules and regulations, having the fun they never had at the time. The trouble with this can be that it leaves the young person with little sense of safe boundaries or anything to push against; how can he find out who he is separate from his parents if his parents keep wanting to be just like him. Of course parents should have their own share of fun but not expect their teenager to provide it for them all the time. Parents who never felt able to rebel are often unable to allow their teenagers any room for manoeuvre and set rigid and impossible standards, which often lead the adolescent to give up the fight completely because it feels impossible, or alternatively to fight very hard to gain just a little ground in the search for independence.

Even when this phase goes relatively easily, it is important for parents to be together in their handling of their adolescents. If they disagree seriously over limits and demands they will leave the adolescent to fall down in the gap between them, or at the very least to exploit the differences in a way which upsets everyone. It is one of the harder facts of life that children reach adolescence when most parents are feeling ready for a rest after all the years of working both in and out of the home. Just when they long for a quiet life their children reach this turbulent period. As the teenager gets increasingly involved in his world outside home and family, so his parents are confronted with the state of their own relationship and they may not feel happy with what they find. This feeling of weariness and emptiness can add to the difficulty of coping with teenagers. Parents may feel very envious of the young person who seems to be having such a good time. For parents who are facing problems in their own relationship or stress at work, having a stroppy teenager around the house can be the final straw, and it may feel to the teenager and the parents as if it is his fault that they are so unhappy.

Parents who have always been close and companionable with their children, sharing activities and interests may feel empty and useless when their adolescents no longer want them to share in everything. There are all the worries too about behaviour, particularly over sex, drink, drugs, delinquency, etc. Being too restrictive can lead to a stronger rebellion, while being too lax can leave the teenager not knowing where any limits lie. It is helpful if some of these 'hot' issues have been talked about at home in general conversation over the years so that the adolescent feels he can talk to a parent if necessary. It is important to find a comfortable balance between the extreme of parents who seem quite unapproachable on these personal matters and those who are overintrusive, expecting to know all about the details of their young peoples' private lives. How can the adolescent become separate and grow up if his parents are wanting him to be sharing all his inner thoughts as well as all the action! Children need to have the facts about sex long before they become sexually active, from then on they will learn both by example and experience, some of it painful and some of it rewarding and fun. Parents stand on the sidelines and share the ups and downs. They should do their best to control the boundaries, whistle for time to come in, but accept that the game is played out there on the field of life, sometimes exciting and dangerous and at other times tedious and depressing. Adolescents make their own mistakes and learn through them. Parents provide the homeground, set the boundaries, punish offences, make the sandwiches, bandage the damaged limbs or the hurt prides, boost morale, and generally go on caring and not expecting too many pats on the back for all their efforts.

Parents often complain about their teenagers being so unpleasant, rude and critical about everything their parents say or do. This is part of learning to separate. For if parents are all knowing, all wise and all powerful, how can the child ever leave them?

Having an adolescent can feel to parents as if they are attached to him with an elastic band. If the parents remain steady the child can pull away and bounce back safely, but if the parents are unsteady then they will be pulled and pushed all over the place. The elastic stretches and contracts, leaving everyone utterly confused and exhausted with the adolescent still attached. Parents coping with their adolescent child are often amazed to learn that people outside the family see him or her in quite a different light – ghastly at home and a delight elsewhere. It can be hard for the parents to take this when they are the ones who devoted years of love and attention to this resident monster whom no one else recognises. Many parents thoroughly enjoy their children in adolescence. They bring life and colour into the home and the challenging of attitudes and beliefs can be stimulating.

It is during this adolescent phase that parents often seek outside help, usually in the hope that something can be done to their adolescent child to make life tolerable for everyone. But often the adolescent is in fact drawing attention to other issues in the family which may be affecting how everyone is coping during this more turbulent stage.

Eve was 14 when her mother, Mrs K, asked for help. The problem as she saw it was Eve's refusal to come in at an agreed time which had provoked Mrs K to hit her. She felt matters were getting out of hand and she was at her wits end. Mrs K, Eve and David, aged 6, came for a family meeting. I was immediately struck by how old Mrs K looked. She was 47 at the time but looked much more like the children's grandmother. Eve could have passed for 17, she was a lovely girl, physically mature, slightly over made-up but exuding a sort of youthful good health and radiance that was in complete contrast to her mother. David was a wraith of a child, rather pale and thin and extremely shy. Eve had been a longed for baby by Mrs K's first husband who had left her when Eve was one. After a year Mr K came into the family and when David was born he married Mrs K and was the only father Eve could remember. The family stayed together until Eve was 12, at which point Mrs K could no longer tolerate Mr K's long periods of silent ill temper. She and the children moved near to her elder sister and Mr K visited quite amicably though infrequently because of distance. As they told me their story I was aware of the deep bond of love between Mrs K and Eve and was not surprised when both acknowledged the special position each had for the other. Eve was the precious, long-awaited first-born child. Mrs K said, 'She is my beautiful baby, I would like to keep her in a glass cage', but Eve was also her mother's helpmate and supporter. Mrs K had a lot of illness including high blood pressure and she knew she was not good at coping with practical problems. She lent quite heavily on Eve who was a capable and sensible girl.

The other important information was that Mrs K had moved to be near her married elder sister on whom she also depended for support but by whom she always felt criticised and undermined. This sister had one son who was seen as a paragon of virtue who had never disobeyed his mother and like his father, was submissive and co-operative. It sounded as if he had not been able to have an adolescence at all for fear that he upset his mother.

Mrs K was trying to be reasonable about the time for Eve to come in, but she was so anxious about what she imagined Eve was doing when she was out, that she insisted on knowing exactly who she was with and what she was doing all the time and would telephone or even visit the houses where Eve had said she would be. When she discovered Eve had lied, Mrs K was beside herself on two accounts.

Firstly, her adored baby was at risk of pregnancy, drugs and drink, and secondly that Eve's behaviour left her, Mrs K, open to criticism from her sister. In her anxiety Mrs K would try to keep such a close eye on Eve that the girl had to lie to get any privacy. Eve felt awful upsetting her mother and lied about where she was in order to spare her mother from worrying, for Eve knew about the high blood pressure and was really afraid that her mother might collapse one day if Eve upset her too much. Eve was having her difficult 'adolescence' quite early and I suspect that this was partly because she had already been abandoned by two men, her own father and Mr K, and was looking for reassurance about her own lovability. She tended to have boyfriends who were a lot older than she was which was another source of worry for Mrs K.

Eve and her mother identified the main problems and worked together on strategies to tackle them. The first of these was their plan to work out a weekly schedule of times for Eve to stay in and go out. Eve agreed to go home in the evening at the time her mother asked, but Mrs K was not to check up on Eve unless she was late home. Eve would always take 10p so she could telephone if she was going to be late, for they lived in an area where the buses were extremely unreliable. Mrs K planned to include Eve's 19-year-old boyfriend in these arrangements. Secondly, Mrs K would tackle the problem of her relationship with her elder sister. Whereas she previously ran to her for help and then resented her interference, she would begin to pull back from doing this. She planned to talk to her sister, telling her how much she valued her concern but that she intended to manage her children in her own way. Thirdly, but linked to this point, Mrs K had to fill the gap in her own life which had resulted from two failed marriages and would be compounded if she was going to set a limit on her relationship with her sister, and give her daughter some space to be separate. Mrs K was likely to feel lonely and might turn to David to meet her emotional needs. She realised this and resolved to go out more and see people in the day. Instead of being a failure because her daughter was being 'difficult', Mrs K began to believe in herself as a 'good enough' mother who could

tolerate ups and downs and did not have to be totally in control as
her sister was.

Chris was 15, when out of the blue and completely out of character
he was arrested for shoplifting. His kind and loving parents were
distraught and asked for Chris to be seen at the clinic. He had a sister
of 19 who was living away from home and a brother of 22 in
Australia, so Mr and Mrs Cox came just with Chris. They made a
sad picture. Mrs Cox near tears all the time, Mr Cox giving off an
air of permanent baffled concern. The first thing I noticed about
Chris other than his miserable bearing was how out of fashion his
clothes were. He was immaculately and expensively dressed but he
looked oddly out of his time.

I heard that Mr Cox ran a family business and had always hoped
their elder son would carry on the tradition and join his father. They
were shocked and hurt when he announced at 18 that he was not
going to college and was off to Australia. At that time the Cox's
decided to send Chris to a private school in the hope that by, 'mixing
with a nicer type of child', he would conform to their wishes and not
rebel as the elder one had done. Chris had been a good child and had
done exceedingly well at the school. He was not only hard working
but played several musical instruments and was involved in the Duke
of Edinburgh award programme.

I asked about his sister and could elicit little information except
that she too had been a bright child who had dropped out of
comprehensive school at 16, got in with a 'bad crowd' and was
currently in a squat in London with a group of friends. She had not
been home for several months.

Mr and Mrs Cox were not authoritarian or cruel parents. There
was no obvious reason why their children should be wanting to get
so far away from them. They were deeply upset and Chris was very
depressed and could not begin to say why he had shoplifted (by the
time I saw them he had got off with a caution). Although that crisis
was now over it seemed likely there would be others. Either Chris
would do something that his parents said was out of character or he

would stay very depressed. We agreed on a series of meetings to look more deeply at some of the issues that had come up in the first meeting I had with them, the central one being that none of the three children had been able to negotiate adolescence in a satisfactory way.

In the second meeting I heard about the parents' early lives. Mr Cox's father had a serious and deteriorating illness throughout Mr Cox's childhood. From an early age he would help his father in all sorts of ways and left school as soon as he was able so that he could devote more time to helping the family business. He could recall no time when he was rebellious or difficult in any way. His father had died when Mr Cox was 16 and young as he was he took over as man of the house, and at the time I first met the family he was clearly still very committed to looking after his mother who lived nearby and who spent many weekends with the family.

Mrs Cox had an older sister who had always been a 'problem child', rebellious and unco-operative. Mrs Cox had been the 'good' daughter who stayed at home to care for both her parents until she married. When Chris was only a baby Mrs Cox's mother died and her father came to live permanently with them. Shortly before I first met the family he had moved into a geriatric hospital. When I asked Chris what it had been like having his grandfather living with them, he said very little and looked troubled and upset. I sensed I was on difficult ground. Mrs Cox then told me that the old man had been very difficult indeed and she had been quite exhausted meeting his demands, as well as looking after the family. Both Mr and Mrs Cox had felt deeply committed to caring for him but their resentment and anger had been well buried, and they had not allowed the children to moan or complain about their grandfather in any way. It seemed that he had dominated family life for several years and as I heard more about all this I began to understand the children's dilemma. Neither parent had had a normal family life, neither had rebelled in any way. Mr Cox longed for a father who had died too soon and Mrs Cox clung on to her role as the good daughter, unable to face her anger with her father or to deal firmly with him. The children joined in their parents' pretence that all was fine until they hit adolescence and began to want to challenge what was going on. Sensing how much this would have upset their parents, the children had little choice but to leave home or stay and continue the pretence. The eldest two leaving had been a sort of protection for their parents who were clinging on to their view of themselves as carers and copers who were used to making sacrifices. In this context Chris's stealing had jolted them all into looking at what had been going on. Mr and Mrs Cox began to face and share their long buried pain and rage with their own parents. Until they had done this work for themselves there was no way they could tolerate their own child's rebelliousness. It was a painful process but a liberating one too as they reassessed themselves, their pasts and their hopes for the future. It was a tremendous relief for both parents to give themselves permission to be less than perfect. They became more real and relaxed and spontaneous. The phrases that came up again and again were, 'I didn't know you felt like that', 'Well, I didn't want to upset you'. They began to experience how an irritation or criticism shared does not kill the other person off, and that to be loved they need not always be good or kind.

Chris began to gain confidence in himself, expressing his own opinions and making choices which were not always ones that would please his parents. He also began to look more normal for his age, risking styles of clothes and haircut which previously he would not have dared. Some months after our contact ended I had a phone call from Mrs Cox, she wanted me to know of some important things that had happened in the family. Grandfather had died peacefully in hospital and Mrs Cox felt much calmer about this than she had expected. Through the work we had done she had given up feeling so guilty and had faced the real feelings about both her parents and achieved a sort of calm acceptance which had made it possible to say goodbye in an honest way. Then Chris's sister had turned up for Christmas and to everyone's surprise the visit was really successful. She had begun to plan her future which included frequent visits home where she could now be accepted as herself and not have to cover up feelings to protect her parents. Chris was fine, enjoying school and friends though still undecided about whether or not to go into his father's business. It sounded as though he felt he had a free choice now and was not going to be compelled to do something that he did not want to do, just to avoid upsetting his father. Only time will tell, but clearly Chris no longer had to do something out of character to get his parents' attention and there was much more open and real communication between them all.

Many of the worst battles between parents and adolescents are over the vexed question of who is in charge. Younger children may get fed up and angry at being told to do something that they do not want to do and they find all sorts of delaying tactics or even get furious and disobedient, but in the end usually give in to their parents' wishes. The adolescent is much less likely to give in to the parents' demands and is better able to resist and fight.

Mr and Mrs Batley's battles with Fiona, 15, had reached such a level that they were asking for her to be taken into care as they felt that she was quite beyond their control. When I offered a family meeting they were doubtful about Fiona agreeing to join in. I suggested that they put the idea to her in terms of everyone feeling unhappy about the situation, and they as parents were wanting to think about how matters could be improved. This shifted the focus away from Fiona as a 'bad' or 'difficult' girl. Rather to her parents' surprise Fiona agreed to the meeting but only on condition that her younger sister Alice, who was 9, was not present. When we first met, Fiona was dressed to shock and she was extremely argumentative and rude to her parents. She dismissed everything they said as 'rubbish' and told me within minutes that the trouble was that her parents were old fashioned and intolerant and did not let her have her own opinions on anything. She felt they stopped her from doing everything she wanted and made her do everything she did not want to do. From her parents I heard all about Fiona's filthy bedroom, her refusal to do any chores in the home, her unsavoury friends and how she stayed out very late at night. They felt they never had a nice conversation with Fiona and that everything turned into a row.

There were many ways of approaching the problem but the situation was so serious that if nothing changed it seemed likely that a crisis point would be reached in which something dreadful might happen. It was probable that Fiona might run away or do something more self-destructive such as taking an overdose of pills. Mrs Batley felt on the edge of a breakdown and Mr Batley was having chest pains and said he could not concentrate at work. I heard that Alice kept out of the way by playing in her friend's home or in her bedroom, she sometimes seemed frightened of the rows which went on all the time. If the situation had not felt so explosive I might have wanted to explore the parents' backgrounds and relationship. But the Batleys were at war and there was no time to sit round and reflect on these issues. I felt we needed to do something straight away that would be helpful to them all. The first and essential move was for me to ask both parents and Fiona to say whether they really wanted to try to stay together as a family. Even though there had been lots of angry statements about running away and going into care, they nevertheless were all quite clear that they did want to find a way to live together. That being the case, we had to renegotiate the rules and get them written down in the form of a contract.

This may sound a strange idea but it can be very helpful in situations where everything is turning into a battle in which no one knows what is really going on. The contract can be worked out in moments of comparative calm when the battle is not raging. Through discussion and compromise an agreement can then be reached which helps the adolescent to feel part of the rule-making and consequently less put upon. It is much harder to get angry with a piece of paper than with parents. Mr and Mrs Batley needed to think together in some detail about what were the important issues and what were the petty ones that were not worth fighting over. They wrote these down while Fiona listed her complaints and demands. We looked at both lists and worked out a contract which both parents and Fiona signed when an agreement was finally reached.

1 Fiona will stay in on Monday, Wednesday and Thursday evenings.

2 On Tuesday and Sunday Fiona will be in by 10 pm. On Friday and Saturday in by 11 pm or later by prior agreement with Mum and Dad.

3 Fiona will clean and tidy her bedroom thoroughly at the weekends and be responsible for putting her dirty clothes in the washing basket and cups and plates etc. to be washed up daily.

4 Mum and Dad will *not* go into Fiona's room unless they knock first and are invited in. *Mum will never go in when Fiona is not there.*

5 Fiona will not swear in her parents' hearing.

6 Mum and Dad will not comment on Fiona's hairstyle.

7 Fiona will decide whether or not to go with Mum and Dad and Alice to Nan's/church/for a walk.

8 Mum and Dad will accept her decision on item 7 and will not try to make her change her mind.

9 When Fiona is silent Dad will not say 'What's the matter?'

10 Fiona will not ask for extra pocket money.

11 Fiona can spend her own money how she wishes.

Although looked at like this they seemed quite petty matters, they were issues around which the most rows had taken place in the past. It took over an hour to draw up the contract, items were included and then taken out and there was plenty of argument and discussion. At the end of the time I asked each member of the family to say something nice about each other. Mrs Batley said very warmly that Fiona was a generous person who always gave thoughtful presents. Mr Batley said Fiona was good with elderly people. Fiona said that her mum was a 'great cook' and even though they were very old fashioned and strict 'they aren't half as bad as some parents I know'. This made everyone laugh and was the beginning of the slow but real improvement in the relationships between the Batleys. The vicious circle of criticism, rejection and anger had been broken into and the shared work on drawing up the contract proved as helpful as the contract itself, for it provided a forum for reasoned negotiation and a way out of some of the worst rows and disagreements. Fiona was given slightly more autonomy while the ultimate control still lay with her parents. As tension gradually reduced, warmth began to creep back in. There were other issues to attend to and these came up in later sessions. After the initial crisis Alice became involved and we had a number of lively and interesting family meetings. The crucial thing had been to find a way for Fiona and her parents to continue to live under the same roof.

CHAPTER 15

'It's not who gets you born who matters'

Some problems of adoptive families

Adoptive families can have just the same ups and downs as ordinary families, but the factor of adoption can confuse and complicate the picture. Babies placed with adoptive parents in the earliest weeks of life have maximum opportunities to become attached to the parents. How the family settles down together will be affected by several factors, many of which are similar to the adjustments needed when children are born into families, but there are some things that adoptive parents have to cope with which are particular to their situation. Their application to adopt may have come after many years of increasing disappointment over one or the other's infertility. The feelings about this may never have been acknowledged between them or dealt with adequately in the adoption selection procedure. The resentment, disappointment and guilt can affect the parents' feelings towards the new baby and colour their view of problems that may arise later on.

Couples who apply to adopt because of infertility will probably have been through a long period of trying to have a natural child, followed by lengthy and worrying physical investigations and procedures involving a great deal of waiting. They then embark on the lengthy adoption application procedure and more often than not another long period of waiting. The emotional investment in the baby who is finally placed will be enormous. The parents will have been through so much, not least the exhaustive social enquiry, that they often feel they have to do an especially successful job of being parents. Any problems the child presents them with can feel like a major challenge to their confidence and self-esteem. They often harbour an understandable hope that the baby, having been placed so early, will be like them. Everyone knows of adoptive children who end up being more like their adoptive parents than natural children, but there are many families in which the adoptive child is seen to be, and feels, completely different.

Some adoptive parents cannot bear to be reminded that their child is not naturally theirs. As the child grows up and develops his or her own personality, the parents may feel the child is rejecting them. The child then feels misunderstood and undervalued and a vicious circle can be set up which leads everyone deeper and deeper into a world of unhappiness and dissatisfaction.

Alex was placed at 6 weeks with a couple who had undergone extensive investigations for infertility. They were warned that the waiting list for babies was very long but they persisted in their application. After only two months they were introduced to Alex, a beautiful baby, and they adopted him. When he was in junior school they asked for help with Alex who was stealing and lying and was excitable, uncontrollable and altogether too much for his parents to cope with. As the story unfolded and I got to know them better, I felt that whatever sort of child Alex had been they would not have been satisfied with him. They were constantly so critical of him and seemed to focus on all the ways he was different from them. They were unusually quiet, gentle people whereas Alex was highly strung and always on the go. They were well organised and peaceful, he was untidy, noisy and combative. Parents and child made each other feel undervalued and criticised. Alex clearly felt in a 'no win' situation – if he was himself they were not satisfied, if he tried to be what they wanted he was frustrated and explosive, so they would still end up dissatisfied.

One day when I was seeing the parents on their own we went back to the beginning of the story. I heard for the first time in detail of the way in which this couple had been told they could never have children. Both had been investigated and the wife went to the clinic for what she thought were further tests on her, only to be told by the doctor that the cause of the problems was her husband's sterility. She had left the hospital on her own weeping openly, with no one to talk to for the hospital had offered no counselling. She did not want to get into a blaming attitude so protected her husband from her deepest feelings of pain and loss at not being able to have a baby of her own. He felt devastated but so guilty about depriving his wife of a child of her own that he kept his feelings to himself and became enthusiastic about plans to adopt. They were quite unable to talk about their profound disappointment and distress and so having not mourned the loss of their own babies before Alex arrived in their lives, they were unable to feel attached to him, though they were thoughtful and caring parents. Their own unacknowledged grief came down like a sheet of glass between them both, and their relationship with their adoptive son. I am sure that family life would have got off to a much happier start if they had received skilled counselling at the time of learning about their infertility. Another difficulty was the speed of Alex's arrival. A pregnancy of nine months gives the parents time to prepare for a baby's arrival, not just to get ready in a practical sense, although that is important too, but to adjust emotionally to the idea of becoming a threesome instead of a twosome. Adoptive parents often do not know how long they will have to prepare for the new arrival and this can make the beginning phase quite difficult and may lead to problems later on.

All the joys, rewards, trials and tribulations that parents and children face in their lives together have a special dimension for adoptive families. This is particularly so when parents, who have not come to terms with the child not being their natural child, try to turn him into the person they want and not see him for himself. This happens with natural children too, of course, but at least the genetic similarities help this process along. All the love in the world will not make a child something he is not. Even the best attempts at matching are often wide of the mark and some adoptive parents and children have to make enormous allowances for these differences. If we imagine a family like a bed of rose bushes then some adoptive parents try to graft the new rose on to the old stock and it often fails to take. If the adoptive child is seen as a separate rose bush who has been planted next to the parent bush they may all grow happily together leaving each other space to bloom.

Young children are passionate, intense creatures who use their imagination to deal with feelings which might overwhelm them. A child gradually learns that the mother, who sometimes frustrates him by saying 'no' or 'wait a minute' or gets cross, is the same mother who loves, feeds and comforts him. Gradually the 'good' and 'bad' feelings can be experienced in relation to the one important person, and from her to other people and the world at large.

Just as the child has 'good' and 'bad' feelings towards the mother so he may experience her as a 'good' or 'bad' person – in the language of fairy tales the Wicked Witch or Fairy Godmother. Adopted children have an additional hurdle in coming to terms with this tendency to split the good and bad feelings. They have another mother, the birth mother who can be brought into the fantasy to carry the good or the bad feelings which really belong to the real relationships. If the adoptive parents for one reason or another are feeling badly about their relationship with the adoptive child they may not be able to help the child to feel safe with these intense good and bad feelings. The child may then use the fantasy birth mother as the object of love or hate and perhaps fail to integrate these emotions in a real and manageable way. An adoptive mother who is secure in herself and can tolerate her own mixed feelings will not be thrown by the child saying something like, 'You're not my real mummy, I don't have to do what you say.' An insecure, anxious mother may be cut to the quick and feel that the child does not love or value her, she cannot then help the child to feel safe with these strong feelings which may then have to be hidden to protect the relationship. A vicious circle can be set up which distances parent and child and may lead to the child turning inwards to his fantasy life where the adoption can play an important part.

Traumatised children

Some children who are placed for adoption have already, in their short lives, suffered in all sorts of ways. They may have been in and out of care, passed from one relative to another or deprived of basic care and affection, all before they reach their adoptive home. These very young emotionally damaged children can be exceedingly difficult to care for and relate to. They have had so many repeated bad experiences that they may hold back from getting close to anyone lest the rejection occurs again. They may bring their anger and pain into the new family in a way which makes the parents feel as rejected as the child has felt. A whole range of difficult behaviours could result, soiling and wetting, refusing food or eating excessively, biting, scratching, hitting, breaking things, inability to sleep, hyperactivity – the list is endless. All these behaviours though difficult to manage demonstrate that the child is responding and reacting – being alive, and where there is life there is hope. Sometimes even quite young children seem almost to have given up hope, they are depressed and withdrawn and need an immense amount of care and individual attention to come alive enough to show their disturbance and begin to recover from their pain.

It is essential that adopters be given as much information as possible about the child's life so far and not expect to be able to wipe all the past pain away with love and attention. Things will probably get worse before they get better and the healing process may take months or years, certainly not weeks.

To be accepted as adoptive parents in the first place requires a high degree of staying power and commitment. The selection procedure is often very daunting and time consuming. To get through it and receive the letter of acceptance can feel like a 'gold medal of competence in parenting'. It seems like the end of something important when it is actually only the very beginning.

Older children placed for adoption

These children will have memories of their early lives and the significant people in them. They will have the advantage of being able to talk about themselves and will usually bring to their adoptive families not only memories but possessions or photographs as evidence of their earlier life. Such children have often learnt how to relate to new people in a superficially easy way, but once the honeymoon period with the adoptive parents is over may well revert to more babyish behaviour and make demands from their adoptive families to be treated as much younger children. Adoptive parents need to be reassured that it is often a healthy sign that the child is secure enough to revert to an earlier stage of emotional development in order to make good a loss. It can be hard to tolerate the sort of disturbed behaviour these children may show. Soiling in a 3 year old is hard enough to take but a soiling and wetting 12 year old can be quite a trial. Stealing is a common problem in this group of children and must be seen in the context of early deprivation and loss, not as a delinquent act. The anger felt towards abandoning parents and other people who have let the child down may be vented on the new parents, not an easy thing to bear, especially if the new parents are afraid of failing in the task.

I have often met families coping with this type of problem who believe they are failing when actually it is clear they are succeeding by giving the child the security he needs to get in touch with his deepest feelings, to give expression to them and have them understood so that they can then be put behind, rather than being dragged into future relationships where they will undoubtedly interfere with his capacity for loving and being loved.

Mr and Mrs Evans had already adopted Carl, who was 4, when they applied to adopt again. Trixie was 2 years and 10 months and living in a residential nursery. She was a particularly beautiful child with old-fashioned curls and enormous blue eyes. The attraction was mutual and after a number of visits to the nursery and overnight stays at the Evans' house Trixie was placed with a view to adoption. It was not until Trixie was 6 that the infant school head teacher became concerned about her. She had a meeting with the Evans and all agreed that they were baffled by Trixie and wanted help for her. At that stage she was hardly coping at school, she seemed in a world of her own and had not begun to read or write, she was socially isolated and would upset some of the smaller children by repeatedly lifting them up and dropping them. Her parents and teachers felt that she was often cut off from them, Trixie never cried. Her adoptive parents were often very frustrated by Trixie because they thought she was stubbornly refusing to take in what they were saying and doing, she would seem to listen and respond and then go off and do the very thing they had asked her not to do. I felt they were justified in their worry that Trixie might go off with anyone in spite of the warnings she had been given, or that she might wander into the road without looking.

When I met the family I was left in no doubt of the real affection that bound them all. Mr and Mrs Evans had been through some very hard times but felt that in adversity their marriage had deepened. Carl was doing well and the whole family was involved in community activities from Cubs to bellringing. Mr and Mrs Evans were not parents who expected great things from their children, they were certainly not pushing for academic achievement but they were really worried about what would happen to Trixie if she continued to be unable to take anything in. Mrs Evans often became quite desperate to drive things into Trixie though she knew this was not helping. In our first meeting Trixie told me the name of the nursery she had lived in and mentioned the name of another child she had known there. She enjoyed hearing again the story of how her parents and Carl had visited and liked her straight away. She looked animated as we talked about this and then became quiet and rather cut off from us when her parents were telling me that they knew very little about her early life. I could almost feel the protective wall that Trixie put around herself, it felt impenetrable. Clearly Trixie needed it to protect herself from something, but what? If we could answer this question then Mr and Mrs Evans might be able to help her to lower the wall brick by brick, certainly no one could break it down by force.

I arranged next to see Mr and Mrs Evans without the children. I heard that they must have been given only the barest outline of Trixie's early lifestory. She had married parents who were very young and inadequate and she had been the subject of a Care Order after the Health Visitor had found her severely undernourished at about 20 months of age. Her mother had been admitted to psychiatric hospital. In the nursery she had become attached to a disabled boy, the one she had spoken of in the session. She was very protective of him, so much so that some older children were quite scared of Trixie when she defended him and his toys from all comers. As this was the full extent of the background information known to Mr and Mrs Evans we set about finding out more. I wrote to the local authority who had dealt with the case. They took a long time to reply but in the end sent a four-page summary taken from their files covering their department's involvement with Trixie from the age of 3 weeks.

It was an appalling and tragic story. Trixie's parents were both 17 when she was born and had both been to special schools for what were then termed educationally subnormal children. When Trixie was just 3 weeks old she was admitted to hospital with a bruised and cut mouth. There followed a tragic series of events with Trixie going in and out of care with numerous admissions to hospital for non-accidental injuries and many attempts to reunite her with her parents, whose relationship was breaking down. They had terrible arguments during which Trixie was put in a bedroom with the door closed so that she could not hear them. When it became quite clear that there was no possibility of the parents being able to give Trixie adequate care, she went, at the age of 14 months, to live permanently in the residential nursery. The staff were kind and hardworking but many were very young and there were constant changes. Trixie never made a special relationship with anyone except the little handicapped boy mentioned earlier.

I shall never forget the day when Mr and Mrs Evans sat in my office reading slowly and carefully through this appalling account of their little girl's early life. When they had finished they both had tears in their eyes and Mrs Evans, normally a talkative person, was silent. Then she said, 'We should have known about all this from the start, we could have understood so much about Trixie's behaviour and we would have been different with her.' They were able to make important changes after learning about Trixie's past, particularly in coping with her 'brick wall', for now they could see how all her life Trixie had protected herself from terrible scenes by cutting herself off from them. The crosser Mrs Evans became with Trixie for withdrawing from her, the more Trixie withdrew. Now they could do the opposite and give Trixie the calm space she needed to feel safer to reach across to them. We now understood why Trixie picked up smaller children and dropped them. She was repeating her own experience of being picked up and dropped by her parents, dropped in the sense of not being consistently cared for and probably physically dropped on occasions. She had no experience in her early life of being made to feel safe, to be held on to by a reliable and consistent person. Trixie found it very difficult making even slight changes in her life, hardly surprising in view of all the terrible changes and upsets she had had as a baby. Going off to school is a major step for every child but for Trixie just moving from one classroom to another or having a different teacher for a few days had led her to revert to the closed off manner of her earlier years. It was many months before Trixie felt safe enough to start to cry, but when she did it seemed to her parents as if the pain and despair from years before was at last having expression and Trixie began to appear more real and alive. When her adoptive grandmother died she was deeply and genuinely distressed. The Evans have taught her over the years that it is safe to love and be loved. Changes will always be difficult but as she manages each one with the support of her parents she builds up her self-confidence and moves further from the nightmare of her first two years of life.

Laura, who was 7 when I first met her, had spent her first three years in a residential nursery in the Far East, having been abandoned by her mother who left her on the steps of the home. Her English adoptive parents were working in the same country and for many months had been hoping to adopt a child. They were about to set off on a world tour before returning to England when they were told Laura was available for adoption and they could visit her. They were shocked by the conditions in the nursery and even more surprised when they were encouraged to take Laura with them after just two brief outings. Laura spoke only Chinese and had never lived in a family. She picked up English in a very short time and made a remarkable adjustment to a totally unfamiliar situation.

She is an extraordinarily appealing child, bright and articulate with a vivid imagination. Her adoptive parents found her an exhausting little girl particularly at night when she could not sleep and danced around her room singing, playing and reading. Her teacher said that she was easily distracted and prone to annoy others who wanted to concentrate. The more people there were around her, the more excited and difficult Laura became. When she was on her own with anyone she was calm and relaxed and related well to the other person. Her parents had had no help at all in understanding her difficulties and were becoming as exasperated as her teachers. Her mother was particularly angry with Laura for hoarding food. The bottom of her school bag was always full of dried up sandwiches and cake crumbs and she would frequently take food from the larder or fridge and hide it in her room. When her parents asked her why she took it, she looked blank and said she had no idea.

Food matters to us all, it is the means of survival. An infant cries with hunger and is fed, she feels content and with repeated good experiences that her needs will be met and that the outside world is good, so she feels good inside. Trixie and Laura did not have this good experience. In fact, Laura's early months were spent lying on the floor waiting for hard-pressed, unqualified nurses to give her something to drink and eat. The orphanage was underfunded and overstretched, and Laura learnt from the earliest months not to expect anything good to happen but to snatch and hold on to anything that came her way. She had no one to hold her and comfort her or make sure she had what she needed, but she learnt how to survive in a group. Hoarding food was like an instinct born from the necessity to keep herself alive. The conscious memory of actually being hungry had long since gone, but the deep down drive to cling on to whatever she needed in order to stay alive had remained in her unconscious and led to her squirrel-like hoarding of the food, which she hardly ever ate.

Laura's mother regularly checked under her daughter's pillow for bits of food. One day instead of food she found a piece of screwed up paper. It was a poem that Laura had written and it conveyed most poignantly her sense of knowing how it feels to be starved of love and food.

> If God is not there
> Who will care
> If we are good
> He'll give us food.

It took Laura several years to learn that her parents' love was not conditional and that she would be fed and loved even if she was naughty. Wasting food was something that Laura's mother did not like, so she came up with a creative plan. She would check for old food once a week and then she and Laura would go together and give the food to the birds.

Laura would day-dream and talk to herself while she acted out her inner thoughts and fantasies. She liked her mother to sit with her while she had a bath. At these times her mother felt that Laura was telling her something important and yet sensed that she should remain quiet and not intrude by comment or question. Over many months Laura would talk of her imagined real brothers and sisters and her natural mother, of how they were playing together in the hot sun in their far off country. Her natural mother was a princess in flowing dresses and jewels. Laura wove elaborate stories around these 'family members' occasionally looking up at her mother to tell her what was going on. I think she was making sure that it was safe to have these thoughts and her mother's quiet acceptance of whatever Laura told her made Laura feel secure and whole. When Laura said something like 'I have got ten brothers and sisters who love me very much and play with me every day', it might have been tempting to introduce a bit of reality but what her mother actually said was, 'have you really, that's nice'. One evening Laura looked up and announced that her 'real mummy is dead', she said it calmly and her mother simply replied in a sympathetic voice, 'Oh! is she, that's sad.' Laura looked calm and began to hum, she never mentioned her imagined natural family again. With her mother's help Laura had healed herself of much of the pain that she had had to face. Through fantasy and play she had come to terms with the sadness of her early life and the loss of her natural mother. Now she began to settle and seemed calmer, her teacher no longer felt Laura to be a disruption but valued her imaginative and creative personality.

To know or not to know

Laura's mother had given Laura permission to think about her first mother. It is often difficult for adoptive children to ask questions about their origins for fear of upsetting their adoptive parents, and because the children do not ask, the parents believe the children do not want to know. Imparting information about adoption can be a bit like talking about sex. Parents frequently tell me their children are not interested in the facts of life because they do not ask, but I have never met a child who is not interested in how babies get born and as they get older so they become more and more interested. If they do not ask it is because they sense their parents do not want them to ask. It is often the same with adoption. The longer the questions about the child's adoption are not asked, the more difficult it becomes to ask. There are, at the other extreme, parents who talk about the adoption too much, which can feel very persecuting for a child who wants to get on with his life and feel safe and secure.

There are children for whom being adopted means something so painful and shaming that they try to deny the reality. I once sat with a family with three adopted children, all placed at six weeks with adoptive parents who had no difficulty whatsoever in imparting information and dealing sensitively with their children's problems and questions, and yet these three children felt quite differently about being adopted. As I helped them to compile a family tree the eldest gazed out of the window with tears in his eyes. He had come to see me with his family because his arrogant superior attitude was antagonising other children and teachers at school. As we touched on the painful feelings around being adopted his distress was obvious. Having refused to join in with compiling the family tree he swung round in his chair and angrily said, 'I don't go back to anywhere or anyone, life begins with me.' His superior attitude was a cover for his deep sense of humiliation and loss. It took a long time for him to speak of these feelings. His sister who was also adopted had a completely different attitude to the whole thing. She had dealt with her sadness of losing her natural family (she knew she had brothers and sisters) by turning it to her advantage. It made her feel special and precious and I remember her delight at discovering that she had eight grandparents if she added up the natural and adopted ones. She loved feeling part of a real life drama. She was fascinated, even when she was very young, by how people are related to each other. She knew more about the family history than anyone else and amazed her parents by recalling dates, places and events which they had long since forgotten. The youngest boy who was only 6 when I first met the family was more interested in collecting cars than thinking about being adopted. He had what facts he needed to understand why his skin was a different colour from his parents and I had no doubt when he was older and wanted to know more he would be told. These three were so different in their feelings about being adopted and were fortunate in having adoptive parents who could respond sensitively to each child's different need to know about their origins.

Adopted adolescents and their search for identity

'Who am I?' is the crucial question in the minds of all adolescents searching for an identity and sense of self, but it has a special meaning for adopted children. Even if they have been given all available information, they will still wonder about the 'lost' parents. Many adopted parents harbour dread that one day their child will choose to leave them and go in search of the birth parents. This fear can be very real when relationships come under the stress of adolescence, with all the challenge and rebellion that belongs to that period of family life. When parents seek help at this stage it is often because they feel very muddled about how much significance to give to the fact of adoption. All sorts of unspoken hopes and fears surface in the minds of parents and children, which interfere with the way everyone relates.

When a 15-year-old adopted girl asked her adoptive mother if she could show her the documents relating to her natural parents, her mother reacted by feeling this was the beginning of the end. The girl was going through a difficult and moody phase of adolescence and her parents saw her request for information as the proof that she did not really love them and that they had failed. The girl, who loved them very much, sensed their insecurity and protected them from their distress by hiding her wish to search for information, which she then had no choice but to carry out secretly.

Another family came for help when their 14-year-old adopted son, David, was brought home by the police, who had found him lying very drunk in the middle of a road. His parents were distraught and feeling quite helpless. He knew what little facts there were about his birth parents. That they had been married, but the man drank heavily and was violent towards his wife, who had felt unable to care for another baby. David's adopted parents held to their belief that he had inherited his bad character from his birth father, so avoiding the painful realisation that it was they who could not cope with a testing out teenager. David was struggling to find out who he really was and the experiments with drink seemed to reflect his attempt to identify with his own lost birth father. What he needed most of all was a chance to talk about his confusion and anxieties with his parents and for them to behave like the parents of any testing out teenager – to set limits and carry on caring and being there, not giving up and leaving him to clutch on to his only lifeline, an identification with a drunken father.

Earlier I stressed how important it is for adoptive parents to have come to terms with their own infertility. This can become an issue when their adoptive child enters adolescence and begins to develop into a full sexual person. Some adoptive parents become very restrictive and intrusive, wanting to know where and when and with whom their teenager spends time. I have met a number of families where this was happening. On the surface the parents felt that they would be judged as having failed if their adoptive child got off the straight and narrow. Deeper down was the fear that the child would repeat the birth mother's experience and through casual sex become pregnant. Buried even deeper in the parents' unconscious was the envy of their adolescent being young, attractive and having the possibility of creating new life. These are not easy or comfortable feelings to explore and put into words, but the parents who made efforts to talk to each other and to their adoptive children about these buried feelings felt that relationships improved and deepened. The ups and downs of adolescence were less alarming and they could all survive. Others were not prepared to look at these issues, and could not allow their children to do so either. In their desperate wish to control everything and deny inner thoughts and feelings, they built a wall between themselves and their adolescent children, sometimes leading to a complete split and mutual rejection.

Janice was one of the angriest teenagers I have ever met. She drove her adoptive parents frantic with worry and battled on every front.

They were responsible and caring people, rather old fashioned in their expectations of teenagers, who managed to survive the tests she gave them – swearing, drunkenness, pregnancy with termination, VD, running away and so on. They never gave up on her, even though they often believed that she had given up on them. At 16 she told her mother she wanted to contact her birth mother. Her mother told me later that at that moment it felt like the ultimate challenge, as if Janice was saying, 'I have tried and tested you in every way, now I have brought out my final challenge, are you going to give up on me, like my first mother did?' Her adoptive parents took the view that she was entitled to know about her origins, even though this was upsetting to them. They also knew that if they refused to help her, she would go and search on her own. So they helped her and for various reasons Janice's birth mother was quite easily found. They met on a number of occasions. Janice found out all she wanted and then settled down. A year later the local newspaper ran a feature on adopted children and there was Janice's picture and an interview in which she said she realised what a problem she had been, that meeting her birth mother had been a disappointment but also a help, because she could now appreciate all that her adopted parents had done for her. I think Janice's parents would have had problems with their first teenager, whoever it had been. Their rigid and old-fashioned attitudes certainly contributed to Janice's problems but the factor of adoption made it much more complicated for them all. They were prepared to look at their part in the difficulties and plan ways of dealing with Janice. They held on, sometimes only just, through thick and thin and were always there for her to come back to. They got her through and she knew it and through the columns of the local paper, she made a public acknowledgement of their love.

Natural families and adoption

Even with the most skilled preparation and discussion with other adoptive parents and social workers, the impact on a family from taking in another child who is going to stay cannot really be understood until it is experienced. Adoptive parents and their children are motivated by genuine feelings of wanting to love and help a stranger. Inevitably there will be a fantasy of rescuing and healing the innocent victim of other people's failures. It is therefore an awful blow to many families when they are put in touch with feelings of hatred and despair. It is particularly hard for parents to see their natural children's lives being upset by the newcomer. All sorts of problems arise over sharing, status and special treatment. The early weeks may be easy while everyone treats the new situation with enthusiasm and sensitivity and patience, but as the child begins to feel more secure he may test out the limits in all sorts of ways. The adoptive parents' central dilemma is often around the issue of how much to treat the child as special and how much he needs to be seen as just the same as everyone else. The frequently heard complaint of brothers and sisters is that their parents let the adopted child get away with things that they would be punished for. Parents need to establish ground rules for behaviour, family routine and natural domestic justice so that the adopted child can learn how the family ticks and so join in. As in all families there are bound to be times when allowances have to be made and special understanding given to a particular child. An adopted child may need this more often.

I think it is crucial for everyone in the family to feel that it is OK to get fed up and upset about the changes that inevitably occur when an outsider joins the family. It would be extraordinary and worrying if they did not. It is all part of living closely together and finding ways of relating that lead to a deepening of commitment and the growth of love. If the angry, upset and hateful feelings have to be repressed because everyone is trying so hard to be nice, then the positive, warm, loving feelings will be held in too.

The hardest question

Adoption can be a deeply rewarding and enriching experience for everyone involved but it does not work by magic. Good intentions are only a tiny part of it, love cannot conquer all. It often takes and needs a hefty dose of blood, sweat and tears as well. It was a boy of 9 who said in a family session, 'It's not who gets you born who matters, it's who loves you.' He had been finding it very difficult to come to terms with being adopted, particularly as the other two children in the family were born to the parents. Of course it matters who gets you born and it mattered to him very deeply, but when he said these words it was an acknowledgement that getting born was only part of it, and that love is something which grows between people and comes from the day to day experience of caring and sharing. He had had to face his sadness that he had not grown inside his adoptive mummy's tummy. He also had to confront one of the deepest dilemmas of adopted children, the one which touches on the most difficult question of all – Why was I given up? Adults can comprehend the dilemma of the young pregnant woman who may have neither the physical nor the emotional resources to keep her baby, but to a child it goes against all the laws of nature. The explanation that was often given, 'She loved you so much she wanted you to have a nice family to love you' simply will not wash, for if she loved me that much, the child will think in his heart, she would not have given me up. Many adopted children work it out for themselves by believing there must have been something about them which made them unlovable. Time and time again I have sat with adoptive children who are struggling to find answers to this unanswerable question, for whatever the reality, however much the facts remain, nothing short of a mother's actual physical death is a good enough reason for a child to tolerate the thought that his mother gave him away. The sadness and anger has to be faced and shared. This little boy with the help of his family came to terms with this, although like all adopted children he will carry deep inside him the scar, however small, of that first and total separation.

CHAPTER 16

The power of secrets

The word 'secret' has so many meanings and associations. Think of the excitement when someone says, 'I want to tell you something secret – you must never tell anyone else.' Sharing a secret leads to feelings of specialness and intimacy. Then there are secrets which we may wish we had never been told because they lead to distortions and lies and difficulties in relationships. Secrets are so powerful. They bind people close together while keeping others at a distance.

Families have secrets too. Sometimes the whole family shares a secret which is kept from the outside world. Within a family there may be secrets shared by certain members which exert a powerful though unseen influence on relationships and communications. It would be nonsense to suggest that all secrets are bad or dangerous. Parents and children need to have secrets from each other while each member of a family has their own secret thoughts and feelings. Families in which no one kept anything secret would be chaotic and without any boundaries between generations or individuals.

There are secrets in families which lead to problems and this chapter is about some of those.

When the whole family keeps a secret it is usually because of the shame or guilt that would have to be faced if the secret got out. I once met a family in which the eldest son, who had won a scholarship to university, suddenly left his course and moved into a squat in London. He had been the golden boy of the family and no one, particularly his parents, could come to terms with what was happening. They all agreed to tell no one. They had to invent elaborate stories to explain his absence from home, so although the family avoided the shame of the outside world knowing, they suffered from the sense of isolation from people outside, as well as from the misunderstandings and tensions that arose within the family. The younger children could see at first hand that they would have to conform to expectations unchallengingly, or risk being quite cut off from their parents. Everyone was involved in keeping the secret rather than acknowledging the problem and doing something to tackle it.

Keeping a secret of fact is complicated enough. Keeping feelings secret is much more complex and requires an unspoken agreement between family members to keep up the pretence.

The Alland family wanted to take in a foster-child. They went through the lengthy and exacting interviews and were finally accepted by their local authority. After a few weeks waiting in eager anticipation they were asked to take their first foster-child. Before long each member of the family, parents and children, was feeling upset and resentful about the intruder. Each felt guilty about owning such unpleasant feelings and no one wanted to let the family or the foster-child down by saying anything. Everyone struggled on for weeks without admitting the problem, though not surprisingly the foster-child picked up the feelings and became increasingly upset. When at last one of the children told the visiting social worker how much he hated the foster-child, the other family members tried to play down the feelings. Fortunately, the social worker listened to the child and was able gradually to allow everyone to say how they felt. Paradoxically, it seemed that once everyone could talk about the bad feelings they all began to feel better. The strain of keeping the feelings secret was far worse for everyone than anything that arose from acknowledging the negative feelings. From that moment of truth the placement began to be a success and ultimately a source of joy to everyone.

Parents often keep secrets from their children to protect them from pain and anxiety, and there are times when this is appropriate. More often than not children sense when their parents are worried about something, and they may imagine all sorts of things, some of which are even worse than the truth.

It is difficult to know how much to tell children when someone they love is seriously ill and may die. This often comes up in families when elderly grandparents become ill. The grandparent/grandchild relationships can be a particularly close and important one even in families where the parent/grandparent relationship is problematic. If children are protected from the truth they have no chance to share in the sadness and be helped to face their impending loss. If parents are worried and preoccupied but their children do not know why, they may react by becoming demanding and difficult just when the parents can least cope with extra demands. Children need to know what is going on and to have opportunities to talk to their parents about their fears and worries. They should not be falsely reassured but have their questions answered simply and honestly. There is no need to protect children from grief for strong feelings and tears are part of a child's natural vocabulary. Parents sometimes say they are afraid their children will be made more anxious by seeing their parents weep. But if the sorrow can be shared so can the comfort and the recovery from grief.

It is frightening for children to discover that a loved person has suddenly disappeared without warning. If it can happen once it could happen again and so a child may become clingy and anxious. The secret which is kept to protect the child will, in the end, cause more long-term distress.

Many adults who seek help with emotional problems discover that the underlying cause of their pain is a death or separation which occurred in childhood but was not dealt with at the time. The adults kept secrets from the child who then had no way of coming to terms with events or the associated feelings. The child grows up into an adult who is carrying an unseen burden of unacknowledged distress which can interfere in all sorts of ways, with the adult's emotional life.

A secret in the present

Deciding how much and exactly what to tell children about important family matters will depend partly on each child's age and stage of emotional development.

When Mrs Adamson telephoned the clinic she was very worried about the best way to tell her two children that she and her husband were getting a divorce. She was not sure at that stage whether to take up my offer to meet her and Mr Adamson to discuss the problem fully but we had a long telephone conversation. From the way she spoke I had the impression that her children must be quite young when she suddenly said that she was desperately worried about her son, Adrian, who was glue sniffing. She then revealed that he was nearly 16, while her daughter, Joy, was just 14. Adrian was not only glue sniffing but drinking excessively and had been picked up by the police on suspicion of being involved in a break in at a local factory. I suggested to Mrs Adamson that she should tell her husband about our conversation and they could then decide whether to come and talk over the problem either with or without the children. Minutes later she phoned back to say that she had not really told me the whole story. The truth was that she and Mr Adamson had actually been divorced for over a year but were continuing to live in the same house. She was quite adamant that the children did not know about this. Mr Adamson was away most weekends, the excuse being that he was working and although they hardly ever spoke to each other there really was not a bad atmosphere in the house. They had wanted to protect the children from upset and could see no good reason to tell them the truth.

It was two weeks before I met Mr and Mrs Adamson and then I heard that following our phone conversation they had sat down with both the children and told them the truth. Adrian and Joy had both said that they had known all along having heard arguments late at night, seen letters from solicitors, and overheard numerous telephone conversations. Adrian had always been very close to his father and had been perplexed by his absence from the family every weekend.

He had not believed the story about working and had imagined his father had a girlfriend. He was deeply moved when his father wept telling him of his loneliness at weekends and the strain of living a lie. Once the whole situation was better understood the family could think about a future in which the parents' divorce could be openly acknowledged and around which plans could be made. Mr Adamson found a flat and Adrian and Joy helped him move and made plans to visit at weekends. Then another secret could be brought into the open. Mrs Adamson had been seeing a lot of a man she hoped one day to marry. Because of the pretence that she was still married to Mr Adamson, she had given Adrian and Joy all sorts of fanciful reasons why she was seeing this man. It was a great relief to everyone to stop the pretence. Adrian stopped glue sniffing and cut down on his drinking. He felt less depressed and confused and cut off from his parents. The secret which had been designed to protect everyone from pain had led to much greater upset for everyone.

A secret from the past

The Adamsons are an example of where certain members of the family decide to keep something secret. In Sonia's family, no conscious decision had been made and yet a secret was having a powerful influence on relationships. Sonia was 8 and described by her mother as 'impossible'. Everything was a battle, whereas Brian, 6, was 'absolutely no problem'. At the first family meeting Sonia's father pointed out that he and his wife did not agree about managing Sonia and he wondered if his wife was too controlling with the child and so provoked a lot of scenes. I said that it sounded as if Mrs James was very protective of Sonia. She said she had to be because she could not bear to think of anything happening to Sonia. As she said this her eyes filled with tears and I knew I was in the presence of some tremendous sadness. Mrs James then told her family for the first time how one day when she was only 11 and the eldest of four children, she had been put in charge of her brother of 9 and sister of

7 while the adults were working the fields at harvest time. It was hot and sunny and the children walked down by a river, hiding behind trees and jumping out. One minute they were all there and the next minute the little girl was gone. Mrs James recalled the horror as if it were yesterday. She remembered the child's body being taken out of the river and the dreadful sense of guilt, made worse by there being no one to talk to about it. Her parents were in a state of shock and although they never blamed her openly, she had always felt that they thought it had been her fault. No one ever spoke of the dead child. I asked what her name had been, 'Sonia' came the answer. For the first time since that ghastly day so many years before Mrs James was able to share her pain and sorrow and guilt. Mr James had known his wife had a younger sister who had drowned, but he had never heard the full story. We were all deeply moved. The effect on Mrs James's relationship with Sonia was startling. No longer was she seeing Sonia as a recreation of her little sister Sonia. She could start to see her as separate and different.

In facing the feelings about her sister's death, Mrs James also spoke of her resentment with her parents for giving her so much responsibility at such a young age, and her parents' failure to help her to face her feelings over her sister's death. She could see how the rows with her daughter had given expression to angry feelings that belonged in the past, with the result that the fights and battles for control with Sonia got back in proportion and became manageable for them both.

When to tell

Some family secrets glue together people who would be happier apart, while other secrets keep people apart who would prefer to be closer. Exposing a secret can lead to surprising results.

The secret in the A family was that Mr A was sexually abusing the eldest of his three daughters and threatened to kill her if she told anybody. Mrs A had sensed what was going on but said nothing.

The family were well known in their local community and pillars of respectability. After two years the eldest daughter told her teacher and the police and social services acted immediately. Once the secret was out the family became 'unstuck', the mother divorced the father, something she had been too frightened to do before, and the youngest sister revealed that she too had been abused. Both the girls were offered counselling to help them to begin to come to terms with their dreadful experiences and to face the complicated and painful feelings around the whole problem. Nothing could have changed without one member of the family telling the secret and it had taken enormous courage to do this for the risks involved were great.

The secret that wasn't

At the other end of the spectrum of secrets lies the Blare family. Jason was 15 and referred by the school because of his disobedient and unco-operative behaviour. He was particularly difficult with male teachers. The referral letter stated that he lived with his mother and stepfather. I wrote to the family and in due course we met. I made what turned out to be an amazing mistake in the first moments of the session. I introduced myself as usual and then said that I could not remember exactly what the school had said but I knew that one of his parents was a step-parent. There is nothing very unusual about having a step-parent so I was completely thrown by what happened during the next few moments. First of all, there was what I think is best described as a pregnant pause. No one said anything, I looked from one to another and then Mr Blare said, 'We knew we would tell him one day, but perhaps it is better for it to come out now.' Then I realised that, unknown to me, I had been in possession of an important secret. Mr Blare explained that he was not Jason's natural father but had met Mrs Blare and Jason when Jason was 2. He looked upon the boy as his own son. This revelation had a startling effect on Jason. Far from being upset he looked relieved and in an indefinable way, happy. He simply said, 'It all makes sense now.'

Later he explained that he had always felt there was a barrier between himself and his dad, that he had resented him and wanted to fight him. He had no actual memories of the time before he knew Mr Blare and yet deep down there was a feeling memory of an intruder who had to be fought off and challenged constantly.

I could not help wondering about who else knew this so-called well-kept secret. It then emerged that lots of people knew and some had even spoken of it to Jason. His natural father had remarried and lived nearby. His two sons were in fact in Jason's school and the physical resemblance had not gone unnoticed by staff and children. Then Jason told his parents that he thought he had often seen his natural father and knew he had other aunts and uncles and grandparents and he even knew where they lived.

Jason did not want to rush off and find his lost relations, he just wanted to know how he fitted into the world, who was who and where he really belonged. He was very deeply attached to Mr Blare and now that neither of them had to pretend they were natural relatives, they argued less and got on much better. Jason stopped picking fights with the male teachers and everything at school calmed down.

Secrets certainly can be powerful and often end up causing the very confusion and distress that they have been designed to protect people from.

CHAPTER 17

'Re-entry problems'

The hazards of orbiting in space are as nothing compared to the dangers of the launch and the re-entry into the earth's atmosphere. When family members go away and come back similar problems can arise and a lot of heat and hurt generated, which can be avoided if the issues are faced and dealt with openly. In some families there are daily upheavals arising out of the return of one or other member from work, or school. A parent may be working away for short or longer periods. Then there are the problems caused by the re-entry of older children, who are studying or working away for long periods but who return to the fold at regular, or more likely, irregular intervals.

Absence really does seem to make the heart grow fonder. Home and family become idealised when there is no opportunity to experience the reality of all being together. Servicemen and women, prisoners and children at boarding school, who have to live apart from their families, tend to cling on to a view of family life which becomes increasingly distorted with time. There are many parents who can vividly recall the impact on their childhood and family life of a father who returned from the Second World War after years away. These men came back into family life as strangers to their young children, and all sorts of difficulties and disruption arose which are still affecting those families today.

Just coming in from work

The Careys were having a worrying time with their daughter of 11, Ann, who was locked into an angry and fraught relationship with Mrs Carey. Mr Carey could not bear the rows between them and had decided the best action for him to take was to 'jolly' Ann out of her bad moods by chatting to her and ignoring the rows. Mrs Carey felt excluded and misunderstood, which made her even angrier. She explained that the worst moment of the day was when her husband came home from work. He would come in through the back door into the kitchen, where she was usually busy preparing a meal. He would never stop to speak to her but would go to find Ann and ask her how she had got on that day. Mrs Carey said, 'It was as if *I'm* the difficult child, and Ann the long-suffering parent. It makes me furious.' It was obvious that the relationship between Ann and her mother could not improve until both parents could be seen to be pulling together. The first moments of Mr Carey's re-entry into the family were crucial and set the tone for the rest of the evening. I asked Mrs Carey if she would think of a way of changing the situation so she could feel less angry. After a little thought she said that it would feel much better for her if her husband came to her first and asked about her day. Then she blushed and looking embarrassed said that she would like it if her husband would come and give her a kiss. Mrs Carey was not used to asking for anything and so her request represented a very positive step forward for her. Mr Carey for his part was surprised and pleased with her suggestion and then revealed that he had always thought that she ignored him when he came home and that she did not want his company – a bad case of misunderstanding. It may sound rather artificial to suggest that changes in behaviour will lead to changed feelings, but it can work and it did for the Careys. Next time we met they were much happier. Mrs Carey said, 'I knew he only kissed me because we agreed he would, but it made me feel much better and we had a good laugh about it. I really cheered up a lot.' Mr Carey said that he liked it much better this way and both of them realised it was important for

Ann to know that their relationship was intact, in spite of her demands.

The successful businessman and
the sad angel

When one parent is frequently away, even for short periods of just a few days at a time, all sorts of difficulties can arise for both parents and children. The parent who stays at home may feel abandoned and upset at having to shoulder all the responsibilities. The one who goes may feel cut off and lonely. Life in hotels and strange places can be anxiety-provoking and brings a longing for security and home and family. Children too have feelings about separations from a parent and may be well aware of the emotional and organisational adjustments that have to be made when a parent comes and goes.

Mr Duffy was a successful businessman who travelled extensively in the course of his work. Although he was never away for more than a few days at a time, he often had to go at short notice and could not always be definite about when he would return. The Duffy's had two children, Helena, 10, and Marcus, 5, and the family came to the clinic because Marcus was prone to outbursts of rage which Mrs Duffy found impossible to manage.

At our first meeting I was struck by Mrs Duffy's apparent acceptance of her husband's unavailability. She said she had known when she married him that he worked very hard and she appreciated the high standard of living which this had brought them. The children were composed and polite and it was hard to believe that Marcus ever had a tantrum. I heard that his outbursts rarely occurred when his father was at home and Mrs Duffy had interpreted this as proof that Marcus did not love her as much as he loved his father, which had undermined her feelings of self-worth as a mother. Part of the way through the first meeting I asked the family who would scream and have bad tempers if Marcus were to give them up. Helena and Marcus grinned at the thought and looked fleetingly at their mother. Mr Duffy stared at his shoes. After a moment Mrs Duffy laughed and said she knew she was often irritable, but that was because the children were a handful and she had to cope with everything because her husband was so often away. I took a bit of a risk at this point and said that I felt that there might be a family scream and Marcus had taken on the important task of expressing it on behalf of them all. Marcus could not possibly give up this vital activity unless everyone in the family could acknowledge their own scream. This seemed to make sense to Mrs Duffy who picked up the theme and said how often she got irrationally irritable with the children when really she was angry with her husband. When he came home she wanted a happy family atmosphere and so she had to squash down these angry feelings. I asked Helena what her scream, if she had one, would be saying. She thought for a while and then spoke rather in her mother's defence, saying she knew her mother felt sad that dad went away so much. But did she, I wondered, have her own sad feelings? At this point in our conversation Helena slumped back in her chair and with tears in her eyes looked directly at her father and said, 'Do you remember the Christmas play when I was an angel and you should have seen me, but you went away, that made me very sad.' Her parents looked at each other in obvious surprise and told me that it was years ago, and fancy Helena still thinking of that. Marcus then chipped in to say in quite a cross voice that his father used to take him out to play football but he never does now.

By now poor Mr Duffy was unable to opt out. His family were making clear statements about how much they all missed him and how sad and cross they all felt. I wondered what he was feeling. 'I really had no idea they all felt like this,' he said. He went on to say that he was fed up with the overwhelming demands of his multinational company, but could not see a way out at present. There were all sorts of difficulties with the business and he was the only one who could sort them out. At this point Mrs Duffy said, 'But you never tell me about these problems,' and he replied that he did not want to burden her any more and often made a conscious effort not to talk about anything connected with work. Mrs Duffy smiled very lovingly at him and turning to me explained that now she understood why her carefully planned candle-lit dinners which she prepared whenever he came home were always a failure, 'We are so polite and nice to each other that we don't communicate at all. I have come to dread those evenings.' 'I know what you mean,' said her husband, 'they ought to be a pleasure but somehow it all goes wrong between us.' As they began to talk the children picked up pens and a large piece of paper and started to draw at each end of it. They were sharing the pens and obviously enjoying being together as brother and sister. It was as if Helena was demonstrating that she no longer had to take over the role of mother's support and comforter and Marcus could stop being the mouthpiece for everyone's frustration. To reinforce this new position I suggested the next meeting should be just for the parents without Helena and Marcus.

When the day came Mrs Duffy arrived on her own. My heart sank because I sensed that she was, yet again, carrying all the responsibility for the family. She pre-empted these thoughts by saying that she had only called in to explain that they could not keep the appointment because her husband had been called away late the previous evening. She said she would have really liked to talk to me about a number of things but she felt it important to wait until they could come together. I agreed with her completely and she went away. Several weeks passed before we could meet and that brought home to me how much waiting the family experienced. I could also share their sense of never quite believing that what had been arranged would actually take place. But then one day we had our meeting and it was productive and moving. They said nothing about the children but focused entirely on the problems to do with what we came to call the 're-entry' period. Both Mr and Mrs Duffy felt it was a major problem in their family's life and underlay their sexual difficulties, which Mrs Duffy defined as her husband not wanting her any more while Mr Duffy saw it as his wife's rejection of him. In the meeting with me they were so polite and nice with each other that I began to feel a scream building up inside me. I shared this feeling with them and suggested they might risk telling each other how they really felt. Gradually they loosened up and began to speak directly to each other and not through me. As the emotional tone was intensified this screaming feeling inside me went away. They spoke of their feelings about the job, of the separations and the longing to be together, their efforts to please each other which seemed so often to fail and their shared distress about the lack of physical love. Each wanted to be close to the other yet anger and guilt were getting in the way. They had tried so hard to make things come right but the harder they tried, the worse it got and they had needed Marcus's scream to alert them to their own unexpressed feelings. The airing and sharing of these powerful emotions was an immense relief for them both and really freed them up to get back in touch with the loving, appreciative feelings which they both knew lay behind the distress. They could reach each other again.

We only needed three meetings, the last one included the children, so the family was complete again. Mr Duffy had booked a holiday and made a point of saying that this year he would not allow himself to be called back from it. Although he continued to go abroad frequently, his homecomings were more relaxed and low key. He would ask what they had all been doing and when Mrs Duffy wanted to hear the details of his work and travels he would tell her. They were less formal with each other and I could sense that Mr and Mrs Duffy had rediscovered the joy of being more spontaneous, open and intimate.

The faraway father

Mr Hughes was away for several months at a time on an oil-rig on the other side of the world. Mrs Hughes worked and looked after their three children, Martin, 15, Joanne, 13, and Donald, 11. Mrs Hughes telephoned in some distress asking for someone to see Martin and Joanne 'to talk some sense into them'. I asked who else was in the family and she quickly said that she did not want Donald to be involved – 'he is a good boy, no trouble and I don't want him drawn into it all'. From the information she gave I had no sense of their being a father around in the family. I asked where he was and Mrs Hughes said he was away more than he was at home and was not due back again for six weeks. When I suggested a family meeting she said she couldn't wait for him to come back and even if she did it would not make any difference, 'It gets worse all round when he is here', she said. She explained that Joanne was out of her control, staying out too late and being rude and unco-operative at home. Martin tried to deal with her but he got very down in the dumps a lot of the time and was doing badly at school. It all sounded chaotic and unhappy. I talked to Mrs Hughes about including Donald. I spoke of how upset in one family member is always felt by everyone and even quite young children can be very helpful when it comes to sorting out difficulties and worries. She reluctantly agreed to include him and so I arranged to meet the family the following week.

I took great care to put six chairs in the circle but when the family came in it was Donald who said at once, 'I suppose that's dad's chair, isn't it?' Martin sat slumped in his chair and Joanne looked cross and gave out all sorts of unspoken messages that she did not want to be at the meeting. She sighed and rolled her eyes at the ceiling with an expression of total boredom. Mrs Hughes sat glaring at me as if to say, 'You're the expert, so do something.' I began by asking if they knew why they had come. Donald said, 'Because Joanne is naughty.' Joanne said, 'Shut up, idiot.' Martin kicked her and when she looked as if she might hit back, Mrs Hughes leaned forward and pushed Joanne down into her chair. The atmosphere was explosive. Looking at the empty chair I said I was wondering what would happen now if dad was there. Mum replied, 'They'd soon stop their arguing. He wouldn't stand for it. They listen to him. But it is easy for him, he comes back, plays the heavy father, goes away and leaves me to pick up all the pieces.' Donald said he liked it when dad was home because they did nice things together and had fun. 'Did the others have fun too?' I asked. 'You can't have any fun at all when he comes home, he stops you doing everything. He is a real spoil-sport.' This was Joanne's comment. Martin continued to slump and say nothing. I asked Donald what he thought Martin would say if I asked him how he felt about dad going away so often. Donald hesitated before replying and thought quite hard about the question, 'He thinks he is dad, he bosses us around, then dad comes home and bosses him around.' Mrs Hughes spoke of the frustration at never getting it right. When her husband was away she had to cope with everything and had plenty of angry thoughts about being on her own. Then when he came home and reasserted his authority she felt furious all over again. Martin was trying to fill the gap left by father and felt humiliated and angry each time his father reasserted his position. Mr and Mrs Hughes disagreed about how much freedom Joanne should be allowed. Mrs Hughes compensated for what she felt was her husband's old-fashioned line with Joanne, but then resented the way that Joanne took advantage of her generosity.

We arranged our next meeting to fit in with Mr Hughes' leave. I had imagined a powerful muscular man, who would dominate and control the family, but into the room came someone entirely different. Quite a small softly spoken man, who seemed genuinely pleased to be there in the middle of his family. We were soon into the whole subject of his comings and goings. He spoke of feeling cut off from ordinary life when he was on the rig and of his sense of never getting back into the family in a real way before it was time to leave again, 'You just have to put up with it,' he said with a sad sigh. He did not like coming the heavy father, but felt his wife looked to him to do something to control the two older children. Mr Hughes spoke of feeling like a stranger in his own family and when I wondered what they all felt hearing this, they began to take the risk of being more open and talked of the ways things went wrong and of how it might improve.

Donald said he looked forward to dad coming home and wished he would never go away. Joanne said she was fed up that he was strict and wished he would listen to her point of view. Martin said he felt his dad couldn't see that he was growing up. He wanted dad to acknowledge the ways in which he took over responsibility for things which dad would normally have done. Mrs Hughes said she knew she was impossible to please. Part of her so much wanted her husband there to share in all aspects of the family life, and at the same time she felt resentful about the way he seemed to want to take over. It made her cross and unco-operative just at the time she wanted to be happy. It surprised the family to hear Mr Hughes' thoughts on the matter. He spoke of his feelings and that he never had time to settle in but was under pressure from them all, in various ways. He had been particularly upset in recent months because of Joanne's behaviour and felt he had to be firm because her mother was too lax, 'I have to get all the disciplining in in a short time so it will last for weeks,' he said. Then Martin said to his father, 'You are away so much you don't realise we are not little kids any more.' He was including Joanne in this statement and she looked pleased to feel that she had her brother on her side and not against her.

I asked the family how they kept dad in touch with their lives and activities while he was away. 'We don't,' was the reply. Mrs Hughes said she found letter writing difficult and in any case she could fill him in when he got back. 'But do you?' I asked. 'Not really,' came the reply. 'Do you find out what has been happening at home?' I asked Mr Hughes. 'Not really, there is too much to do when I get back.' The re-entry was definitely a problem and had to be tackled by all members of the family. We worked on a strategy for this which entailed an agreement from each of them that on Mr Hughes' return they would have a family time at which everyone would fill him in with their news of events, upsets, and the good things that had occurred since he went away. Mr Hughes would not immediately lay down any rules or regulations, but instead he would find time with his wife to talk over these general family issues, so they could present a united front.

I still questioned whether Mr Hughes had to be so cut off from all of them while he was away, but they said they were all poor letter writers. It was Donald who had the brain wave, 'We could send dad a tape of all of us and he could send it back with him on it.' It was a brilliant idea, practical and simple, and it appealed to them all. I asked them each to think about what they would like to use the taped messages for. Mrs Hughes said it would be good to turn to her husband for support and advice, to be in touch. Martin announced that he would make sure dad appreciated all the jobs he was doing for him. Joanne said she hoped he would treat her more responsibly if she told him what she was up to. Donald thought the family dog could contribute something by way of a bark or two!

I met them again after several months. The taped messages had become an enjoyable part of family routine and had led to a much more relaxed re-entry period. Mr Hughes was no longer desperate to get back in and grab hold of the reins. He felt more secure and in the picture, even while he was away, and Mrs Hughes felt closer to him and happier to share things and not feel undermined when he came home. Joanne now had two parents who were pulling together which felt safer for her and resulted in a much higher level of co-operation. Martin got the acknowledgement he had always wanted from his father that he was growing up and was not to be ignored. Donald continued to ask his father to get a different job. The dog got quite carried away with joy when he heard Mr Hughes' voice on the tape and Mr Hughes said, 'It really brings us all close, it is a good feeling.'

CHAPTER 18

Strategies for parents

Anyone who has read this far will, I hope, have acquired some new ways of thinking about family problems. In this chapter I want to identify some of the useful strategies which can make family life and the task of being parents a bit easier.

Talking about worries

Parents who are worried about their child must find time to talk to each other, to share their feelings and explore new approaches to tackling the problem. They should make sure that the child knows that they are aware of the problem and are concerned and caring about it. Everyone knows how often a physical symptom will clear up just when an appointment has been made to see the doctor, as if the knowledge that help is at hand brings about the cure. The same thing can happen with emotional and behavioural problems. The child who is the focus of the worry often feels better and behaves differently just knowing that the parents care enough to take the matter seriously.

Upset in one family member will usually affect everyone else and may be highlighting difficulties within the family group. For this reason it is nearly always helpful for parents to share their worries with the whole family and spend time altogether listening to everyone's point of view and their suggestions for getting over the problem. Even quite young children can be encouraged to make contributions in a family meeting.

The Frazers dreaded car journeys. The three children argued and fought in the back seat making it impossible for the parents to talk to each other. Tempers rose and tension increased so that by the time they arrived at their destination everyone was exhausted or in tears or very angry. Not a good way to start a holiday or have an enjoyable day out. One evening Mr and Mrs Frazer turned off the television, shut the door and told the children that they wanted to talk about improving car journeys because if things carried on as they were there would simply be no more trips. Everyone had a chance to say what they disliked about journeys and then what ideas they had to improve things. One of the children wrote down all the suggestions and together the family drew up a list of 'rules for car journeys'. All sorts of things came out in the course of the hour but most important of all was a shift in responsibility from the parents to the whole family. The youngest child was given responsibility for time-keeping, indicating when people would change seats and when they would all stop for a break. Another child was responsible for gathering up the games that would be necessary to keep everybody happy on the journey. A new rule was instituted for playing competitive games such as 'I Spy', so that it was no longer the one who got the answer who took the turn but turns were rotated around the family giving everyone a chance. Because the children had helped to make the rules they were enthusiastic about keeping them. Instead of having two irritable parents in charge of three irritable children, the family was able to enjoy what had previously been a boring and stressful situation.

Avoiding labels

It is easy in families for individual members to acquire labels and very difficult to get rid of them. Children can get typecast from an early age: 'the quiet one', 'good one', 'the thinker', 'the little mother', 'the naughty one'. A child who does something completely 'out of character' may simply be revealing a part of his personality which he previously kept hidden. One really naughty, tiresome child in a family can be naughty for everyone else so that the rest of the family can bask in smug delight at how easy and good they are. A child can get trapped by a label and find it very hard to get free. For example, if a child tells a lie (as all children do frequently) and his parent says, 'You are a liar', that can feel like a judgement on the whole of him and he may feel far worse than he should. If the parent labels the behaviour and says, 'you have told me a lie', that is a statement which leaves the personality of the child intact but makes the judgement on the one bit of behaviour.

Accepting feelings

No one likes to be told that they do not feel what they say they feel. An adult who tells a friend he is depressed does not want to be argued out of his state of mind with remarks such as 'surely not – not you – you are always so cheerful – you have got so much going for you', etc. Neither does he want his friend to rush into action to be helpful by immediately organising activities to cheer him up. His most urgent need is to be able to talk to his friend about how he feels, to be heard and sympathised with. Then the friend can ask in what way he might be able to help. When children talk to their parents about their worries and fears they too need to be heard, not argued with or dismissed.

John was terrified of ghosts and witches coming into his bedroom. It was no help when his parents told him not to be silly. They had told him a hundred times there were no such things as ghosts and witches, he must just stop thinking about them. If he carried on they would get very cross. It would have been much more help if his parents had listened to his fears in detail and responded calmly by saying that they knew he was afraid even though they had told him there were no ghosts or witches, that *they* were not afraid and when he was a bit older he would not be afraid either. They could then talk about ways to help such as leaving lights on, doors open, not get into an argument about the fears or define them as silly.

Paul was 4 when his baby sister was born. For a few days all went well and then Paul burst into tears saying he hated the baby and wanted her to go away. His mother might have responded by saying something like, 'Don't say that Paul, you love your little sister really, you would not want her to go away would you? You must not say horrid things like that.' What she actually said as she picked him up to comfort him was, 'She does cry a lot doesn't she? Let's put her in her cot and we'll have a story.' This simple statement had in it an acceptance of Paul's wish to get rid of the baby, she did not argue with him or dismiss his feelings but acted on her intuitive understanding of his sense of being rejected.

Katherine at 13 stormed into the room where her father was quietly having a cup of tea and stated that she was 'never going to that school again'. 'O yes you are,' said her father. 'I am not, you can't make me.' 'O yes I can my girl,' and the rest can be imagined! If we could rerun the scene and give her father new lines the outcome might have been very different. For example he could have said, 'You sound upset, what's up?' or 'Have a cup of tea and then tell me what has happened.' Both of these statements accept her angry upset state without arguing with her. They also offer her a chance to talk about the situation. Nothing further may need to be done. Katherine would have been heard and sympathised with and helped to calm down. Of course, if Katherine's father had a history of rushing into action and complaining to the school at every opportunity, she would probably have said nothing at all for fear he made matters worse by direct and inappropriate action. Children often do not need or want parents to do anything about a worry except to listen and sympathise and be aware of the problem, to bear it in mind, not rush into action.

Susan had taken a serious overdose when she was 14, and at 16 said that her parents' concern was just too much to take. If she looked less than radiantly happy her parents asked her if she was worried about anything. It became impossible for Susan to be just ordinarily fed up and unhappy. She had to hide her feelings and put on a front. This sort of overconcern and constant focusing on a problem can feel quite persecuting. It is often very hard for parents to find the right balance between ignoring or dismissing something and becoming overinvolved and overanxious.

Accentuate the positive

We all do better in life when we are praised rather than criticised. Children are no different from the rest of us, but it can become very hard indeed to break into a cycle of blame and criticism and anger. If a child does ten things which make a parent cross and one that pleases, it takes a special sort of patience to resist pointing out or punishing the ten and then to praise the one. Many children get into a position from which they need to be rescued. The naughtier and more disobedient they get, the crosser the parent becomes, the naughtier the child gets and so on *ad infinitum*. Everyone's self-esteem gets destroyed. At this point a parent may need to summon up just enough emotional energy to stop reacting negatively and feed something positive into the system. It helps to count ten before reacting, to swallow the nasty comment or take the angry exasperated edge out of the voice.

For several weeks Stephen, 5, had been driving his parents to distraction by his negative attitude. Everything was a battle and his parents were worn out and angry. His mother said to me, 'If he is like this at 5, what will he be like at 15?' It was clear that a direct request for Stephen to do something would be met by a direct refusal, simply to repeat the request would get nowhere and a row was inevitable leaving both Stephen and his parents upset. What they needed was a strategy which left them in control, avoided the battle and ended up with Stephen feeling more positive. At the end of our discussion Stephen did not want to leave the playroom to go home. His mother said, 'Come on Stephen, put your coat on, we are going home.' The inevitable reply was a defiant 'no'. She felt like saying, 'O yes you will,' but realising that this would lead to a battle she stopped herself in her tracks and with an excited voice held out his coat and said, 'I bet you can't shoot your hands down your sleeves really fast.' Stephen swallowed the bait and put his arms in his coat with a triumphant smile. His mother said, 'That was clever of you.' She did not need to repeat the request to leave the room for Stephen, delighted with his success, was halfway down the corridor.

Being consistent

Being consistent is not about being rigid and inflexible but it is about helping children, particularly very young children, to experience the security from which they can develop their own ability to make decisions, set their own limits and acquire healthy self-control. A familiar scene for most parents is the exhausting shopping trip with young children trailing along getting in and out of the pushchair, constantly asking for sweets, ice creams or crisps. The parents agree to one treat in the hope that this will lead to peace and quiet then minutes later the children ask for something else. The answer is, 'No you have had something', or 'That's enough.' The children's demands become noisier and more insistent. Parents get cross, passers-by stare, children cry. By now the parents are furious and unable to concentrate on shopping and the situation is upsetting for everyone. If at that moment a parent gives in just to get some peace, the children have learned that by keeping up the pressure they will get what they want. They cease to believe that their parents mean what they say and the parents rapidly sense that they are losing control.

If parents are not in agreement about limits, the child can really flounder and, early in life, learns how to play one adult off against another. A lot of angry hurt feelings can erupt and the child, caught in the confusion, can feel unsafe and out of control.

Sharon and her son Dean, 4 years old, lived with Sharon's father who was disabled and unemployed. He loved them both and Dean's arrival had given him a new lease of life. The trouble was that he indulged Dean in all sorts of ways and undermined Sharon's efforts to be consistent with him. If Sharon said 'no' to something and kept her word, grandpa would take Dean on one side and give him whatever he wanted. If she put Dean to bed when he was trying hard to stay downstairs, grandpa would say something like, 'Don't be unkind Sharon, you would not like to be up there on your own.' Try as she would Sharon could not explain to her father why this was all so unhelpful. Sharon understood that he bitterly regretted having been too strict and authoritarian with his own son, Sharon's brother, who had left home at 16. He probably felt guilty and believed he was making amends by being so loving to Dean. He simply could not understand Sharon's position and in the end she had to move out of his house in order to feel in charge of her own child. There was an interesting twist to this particular story, for after a year in her new flat Sharon met Terry. Their relationship deepened and after about a year they were spending most of their time together. Terry was good with Dean but quick to get cross with him if Dean became overexcited or attention-seeking. Sharon found this hard to take and noticed how she reacted as her father had done, taking Dean on one side and giving him what he wanted, telling him on occasions to take no notice of Terry. This resulted in rows between Sharon and Terry and Dean began to be disobedient and difficult. Sharon and Terry decided to sit down and talk about the problem. They worked out much better ways of coping with Dean who soon sensed that they were 'pulling together', which made him feel more secure and generally calmer.

Contracts

Some people think that the idea of having a written contract between family members is ludicrous, others have found it can be a powerful method for defusing a tricky situation. It takes the heat out of the moment by forcing both parties to sit down before the conflict arises to work out a shared strategy to cope with it. Instead of one person against another it becomes everyone against the problem. The contract or written agreement is a shared one and seems to become imbued with a sort of authority of its own which everyone respects. Many families have washing up rotas which are a sort of contract. In some families when members borrow money this can be recorded, dated and witnessed so that no one needs to go through the tedious and irritating arguments about whether it was borrowed or paid back or how much, when, where, etc.

I once knew some parents who felt their three children were turning into square-eyed zombies through an apparent addiction to television. Every time the parents went to try to switch it off there were howls of protest, meals would be interrupted and worst of all there were constant rows about which channel to watch. One day the parents sat the children down and shared with them their plan to keep everyone in the family happy. They got out the next week's *Radio* and *TV Times* and asked each child to mark with a different colour the seven programmes they most wanted to see. Clashes were discussed and bargained over and agreements were made. Rather to the parents' amazement this scheme was a complete success. The set was turned off the minute a marked programme ended and on a couple of occasions one child dealt quickly with another's attempt to see something else by protesting, 'You can't see that, you didn't mark it up.' The rows over viewing simply stopped and a spin-off from this was that the children became more discerning about what they watched, concentrated harder when the set was on and had more time for other activities.

'New Year Resolutions'

Everyone who makes a New Year Resolution does so in the hope of becoming more like the person they long to be. Most resolutions are made in secret and seem to have a fairly short life. There is a family game which uses the idea of New Year Resolutions to help individual family members to make changes. If one person says bluntly to another, 'I *do* wish you wouldn't do such and such', the person on the receiving end of this will feel criticised and attacked. He may retaliate with, 'I wouldn't do it if you didn't do such and such', and so a tit for tat is set up in which everyone feels less like changing their behaviour than before the discussion began. In this game no one is criticised but each person has a chance to reflect on how she or he is perceived by others and in what ways they might like him or her to change. For example, Aaron and Jean and Kevin, 14, and Alison, 11, sit down to play 'New Year Resolutions'. Aaron starts by saying, 'I think Jean would like me to give less time to tinkering with the car and more time to working in the garden', 'I think Kevin would like me to stop asking him each evening how the homework is going', 'I think Alison wants me to stop calling her "petal" especially when her friends are in the house.' Jean, Kevin and Alison can each respond to these suggestions, they may agree or disagree but they will all appreciate Aaron's wish to be sensitive to their needs. If Aaron had simply asked each of them in what way they wanted him to change and each had come up with exactly the same suggestions, Aaron might have felt criticised and defensive and less willing to change. Each member of the family has a turn and not only can it help oil the wheels of family life but it can be very touching and funny too. It is not a game to be played often or it loses its power to change things, once a year is probably enough, which is why I have called it 'New Year Resolutions'.

CHAPTER 19

Where to go for help with family problems

In the first instance, parents may seek help from a variety of professionals in the community who already know the family. These could include general practitioner, health visitor, head teacher, playgroup leader, minister of religion, etc. Each one of these may be able to give advice or counsel. Just sharing the worry can so often go halfway to solving the problem by reducing the anxiety that builds up when there are worries about family problems. As I hope I have shown in this book there are times when the best way to have help is in the context of a whole family group.

The local *Child Guidance Clinic* (or *Child and Family Psychiatric Clinic*)

> This is the specialised resource in the community for family problems and parents should not hesitate to refer themselves, or where it is necessary, ask their family doctor to refer.

Institute of Family Therapy (London)
43 New Cavendish Street
London W1
Tel: 01-935 1651

> The Institute offers training and consultations to professionals but also has a treatment service for families who can self refer by

contacting the Clinical Consultant. Fees are charged on a sliding scale.

Social service department *social workers*, though often overburdened with statutory responsibilities, will work with whole families under stress, particularly when this helps to prevent more long-term problems or family breakdown.

The Family Welfare Association
501 Kingsland Road
London E8
Tel: 01-254 6251

Offers a counselling service to families who can self-refer. No fee is charged.

The following organisations are all committed in various ways to helping families at particular periods in the family life-cycle.

The National Childbirth Trust
9 Queensborough Terrace
London W2 3TB
Tel: 01-221 3833

The NCT is a large charity with branches all over the UK. It aims to help families achieve enjoyment in childbirth and parenthood. Ante-natal classes, support with breast-feeding, and practical help after the baby is born are the most important aspects of their work. As well as giving post-natal support, many branches organise get-togethers for parents and children.

The Pre-School Playgroups Association   (also for information about Mother and Toddler Clubs)
61–63 Kings Cross Road
London WC1X 9LL
Tel: 01-833 0991

Exists to help parents to understand and provide for the needs of their young children. It aims to promote community situations in which parents can, with growing enjoyment and confidence, make the best uses of their own knowledge and resources in the development of their children and themselves.

The Post-Adoption Centre
4 Gregory House
48 Mecklenburgh Square
London WC1N 2NU
Tel: 01-833 3214

This agency provides an information and counselling service for adopted people, adoptive families and birth parents whose child was adopted.

The National Step-Family Association
162 Tenison Road
Cambridge
CB1 2DP
Tel: 0223-460312 (information)
     0223-460313 (counselling service)

This association aims to offer practical help, support, information and advice to all members of step-families (married or unmarried, full-time or part-time, parents and children). Newsletters, booklets, local groups, telephone help-line. National list of specialist family therapists.

The National Marriage Guidance Council
Herbert Gray College
Little Church Street
Rugby
Warwickshire, CV21 3AP
Tel: 0788 73241

The Council has branches throughout the country. Check in telephone directory or ask at local Citizens Advice Bureau. As children's emotional problems are so often a response to marital stress it is important for parents to have access to counselling for their own difficulties. Short-term and long-term counselling is available through the Marriage Guidance Council and fees to cover costs are negotiated.

Exploring Parenthood
Omnibus Workspace
39–41 North Road
London N7 9DP
Tel: 01-607 9647

Founded in 1982 to explore the problems and pleasures of parenthood. Offers workshops for parents led by experts in the fields of family, child, adolescent and adult development. Aims to promote a dialogue and partnership between parents and professionals. Parents are offered help and advice in setting up local support groups and networks.

The Parent Network
44–46 Caversham Road
London NW5 2DS
Tel: 01-485 8535

Established in April 1986 to improve the relationships between children and adults and particularly parents. The network aims:

- to establish a national network of parent support groups to offer practical programmes to parents to help them find new ways to communicate and improve their relationships with their children;
- to train parents to become co-ordinators so that they can offer the programme to parents in their local communities;
- to provide membership services for parents and co-ordinators

with information support, training books and educational materials;

to work with other adults who have contact with children and young people in creating better relationships and improving communication.

Further reading

Bettelheim, Bruno, *A Good Enough Parent: The Guide to Bringing up Your Child* (London: Thames and Hudson, 1987)

Cleese, John and Skynner, A.C. Robin, *Families and How to Survive Them* (London: Methuen, 1983).

Crabtree, Tom, *An A to Z of Children's Emotional Problems* (London: Unwin Paperbacks, 1983).

Crowe, Brenda, *Your Child and You* (London: Unwin Paperbacks, 1986).

Dunn, Judy, *Sisters and Brothers* (London: Fontana, 1984).

Fraiberg, Selma, H., *The Magic Years* (London: University Paperbacks, Methuen, 1971).

Hooper, Anne, *Divorce and Your Children* (London: Unwin Paperbacks, 1983).

Jackson, Brian, *Fatherhood* (London: George Allen & Unwin, 1984).

Maddox, Brenda, *Step-Parenting: How to Live with Other People's Children* (London: Unwin Paperbacks, 1980).